FISHING FOR
WHALES

FISHING FOR WHALES

14 Prospecting Principles for Enterprise Sales

SAM HEMPHILL

TABLE OF CONTENTS

INTRODUCTION

L ike many sales executives, I struggled with the move from small and medium business account sales into large account sales. Landing a whale seemed like an impossible feat. The move was so hard that I became fascinated with how enterprise sales executives, responsible for originating new accounts, succeed. I latched onto any effective techniques. I developed the prospecting principles I detail in this book through trial and error in my own experiences, through observation of successful enterprise sales executives, and by reviewing other books written on the subject. At some point, after having some success, I realized I could share what has worked for me and combine it with the research I had done to create an insider guide that will help others find success the easy way.

There is very little written on prospecting to large accounts. There is a fair amount of literature on selling to large accounts, but those books are somewhat dated. In the Sandler book on enterprise sales, *Sandler Enterprise Selling*, the authors don't give any techniques or actionable steps on how to create new sales opportunities, in their chapter on prospecting, which is representative of other books written on enterprise sales. Most books on enterprise selling either do not address prospecting or they quickly brush over it. How is a person new to enterprise selling supposed to gain new customers? Some of us—I think a lot of us—need guidance on this subject. I needed help and I have heard large account sales executives relay the same need.

This book is all about prospecting to large accounts. It is written for the sales executive moving from small and medium business (SMB) accounts into large accounts. It is also a resource for large account sales management and firms looking for direction on how to establish new accounts in the enterprise space. If you are new to large account sales, you very likely have a lot of questions. Those questions probably include:

- How many prospecting calls should I make?
- Do I need years of industry experience to work with enterprise accounts?
- I have a much shorter list of prospects. What am I doing with my time if I'm not making 50+ calls a day?
- Can I cold call into accounts of that size?
- Which contacts should I be calling on?
- Do decision makers at enterprise accounts ever respond to solicitations?
- How much do I need to know about the prospect? How much should I be researching?
- Can I reach out to more than one contact at my prospect account?

This book will answer these questions and many, many more.

WHAT THIS BOOK CAN TEACH YOU

In this book, you are going to learn how to make the transition from SMB sales to enterprise sales. You will learn how to:

- Understand and apply the value of your solution, in a manner that creates opportunities
- Choose or prioritize prospect accounts
- Choose the best contacts to call on
- Disqualify prospects that waste your time
- Research your prospects
- Determine which contacts and how many different contacts to call
- Prioritize prospecting
- Determine how many calls, voicemails, and emails you should execute
- Customize your messaging to create opportunities
- Use your phone more effectively
- Use written messaging more effectively
- Determine when and where to prospect in person

How to Use This Book

While you can leverage any one of the principles by themselves, it is recommended that you read this book from the beginning. Each principle has value and builds on the one before. In the conclusion, we look at how the first principles build a foundation, and you leverage that foundation to achieve effective prospecting. However, if only one or a few of these principles resonate with you, by all means, jump to those chapters to explore and implement them in your own practice. Here is the list of the prospecting principles for large accounts:

- Principle 1: Know Specifically how Your Solution Helps Customers
- Principle 2: Your Prospect List Should be Diverse
- Principle 3: Prospects Should Share Themes
- Principle 4: Be Eager to Disqualify Your Prospects
- Principle 5: Know Your Prospects in Depth
- Principle 6: Start at the Top
- Principle 7: Do Background Research when Selecting Contacts
- Principle 8: Find Multiple Contacts
- Principle 9: Prioritize Prospecting Above all Else
- Principle 10: Do Less Prospecting
- Principle 11: Customize Every Call
- Principle 12: Use Your Phone to Cold Call
- Principle 13: Use Written Messaging to Compliment Telephone Calls
- Principle 14: Prospect in Person

Be sure to read Section Three, which contains case studies that bring all these lessons together by recounting and examining real sales engagements. These sales engagements were originated using the tactics in this book. Seeing these tactics in action should help you synthesize the ideas here and give you some confidence that the prospecting principles for large accounts do, in fact, work.

Be patient with the repetition of concepts. I use repetition of key concepts in order for you to retain them. I understand that in our culture we like the rapid and simple upload of new information, which can be great, but information taken in this manner can be fleeting to us. I believe the key concepts and tools in this book need to be absorbed, rather than glanced at, in order for the sales professional to successfully transition from SMB sales into enterprise sales.

DEFINITIONS

I am one of those people who insists on clarifying the differences between business development and sales. In the context of this book, however, I use those terms somewhat interchangeably. Sales is something that takes place after an opportunity is created. Business Development is something that takes place in order to create and operationally support opportunities. These two distinct pursuits get blended when it comes to prospecting. It's not always a clean handoff. A business development person employs sales skills. Salespeople do their own prospecting but don't call it business development. Since this book is about prospecting, you could argue I should only be using the term business development. You wouldn't be wrong, but I want salespeople who are responsible for their own prospecting to identify with the book. Furthermore, different industries and companies treat the titles differently.

In Principles 2, 3, and 4, we discuss choosing your prospects. This may not be an option for you because you may have assigned accounts. If you are not able to choose your own prospects, I do think you will benefit from reading through these principles because you can use the lessons therein to prioritize your prospects. Furthermore, you may find yourself in a position to argue for adding or deleting a prospect and these principles will help you with that argument.

These principles are written for business-to-business (B2B) prospecting and not business-to-consumer (B2C) prospects. However, I am sure that in large ticket B2C prospecting, these principles can apply. In fact, I use a B2C example to open Chapter Two.

I use the terms "enterprise," "large accounts," and "select accounts" interchangeably. I believe some sales professionals may have issue with that because it's common to apply special designations to the term "enterprise." Bud Suse addresses definitions of "enterprise sale" versus "complex sale" when introducing his book on enterprise sales, *Closing the Whales.* I'm sure these are valid distinctions, but I will not employ them. In the context of this conversation, there is no need to stipulate a prospect's geographical structure or even employee count. Sales organizations define small, medium, and enterprise or large accounts differently every time. Some label an enterprise account as 500 seats and up—some 1,000 seats and up. This book is about calling on prospects that your organization deems major, select, large, enterprise, or otherwise big.

I use the term "solution" to encompass all types of products and services. This is common. All companies these days are "solution providers." Companies that used to be "value added resellers" are now "solution providers." You may sell hardware. I still refer to this as a solution. A broom is a clean floor solution. A desk is a workstation solution. Using the term solution helps me efficiently refer to all types of services and products that are sold. Furthermore, the term solution is in line with consultative sales jargon, and this book advocates a consultative sales approach.

Some of the examples given and stories related are my own and some are those of other sales professionals. Names and details have been changed to protect interests and privacy.

SECTION ONE: PROSPECTING FOUNDATION

Enterprise sales is more a strategy than an activity game. It follows that you need to spend more time thinking about and planning your moves. When you are new to a company, most of your time is spent learning about your company's solution and your company's ways of delivering that solution. Your job at that time—and throughout your tenure—is to maintain an in-depth understanding of what your company does and why they do it better than anyone else. What makes your company's solution unique? What needs are in the market that your solution can meet? When you start a new role, take time to answer these questions.

When you are new to a sales position, the rest of your time is spent gathering and researching your prospects or leads, contacts, and your territory and industry, if you were assigned them. Prospecting will start once you have a strong understanding of your company's unique abilities and you have developed ideas on how you can help your prospects accomplish their unique needs. Do not call anyone until you have a custom approach for that prospect. To develop that custom approach, you first need to know one, what your solution can do uniquely, and two, what your prospects need. If you are not new to a company or position, stop what you are doing make sure you know one and two.

When you know what your solution can do specifically for each of your individual prospects, you can be a consultant. As a large account sales executive, you truly are a knowledge worker, in that your value is in what you know and who you know and how to apply that knowledge to create value. Software and technology cannot do this. You are not managing a simple transaction, as done in SMB sales, which everyday edges closer and closer to becoming extinct because technology can handle transactional sales. Technology and systems cannot replace the enterprise sales executive because we create ideas and see them through in an intellectually complex, human manner.

CHAPTER ONE: ACCOUNT SELECTION PRINCIPLES

In this chapter, we will cover four principles of account selection. These principles are:

- Know specifically how your solution helps customers
- Your prospect list should be diverse
- Prospects should share themes
- Be eager to disqualify your prospects

You may not get to choose your prospects because they may be assigned to you. Alternately, your manager and the nature of your role may allow you to develop your own targets. It may be that you are given a list of accounts to target or it may be something in the middle—you are given an area of focus like a vertical (industry) or region. This chapter will speak more to those who have the freedom to choose their own target accounts; but, for those who are given a list of accounts, there are some helpful takeaways here. You can use these ideas to prioritize your list and these principles will help you make arguments for cutting and adding prospects from and to your list.

Even before choosing or prioritizing your prospects, you will need to address your grasp of the solution you are representing. There are degrees of competency in which you understand and applies the value of your solution. On a surface level, you can see the overarching applications that your solution provides. Focusing in and looking at more details, you can see more of the details and specifications of the solution. Drill down further and you will see every specification of your company's solution—how it is formulated and why it was created in that way. In large account sales, you don't need to know every detail of what and how your company provides its solutions, but you do need to know what your company does particularly well and specifically how your solution can address your customer's individual needs.

PRINCIPLE 1: KNOW SPECIFICALLY HOW YOUR SOLUTION HELPS CUSTOMERS

Principle 1 is a no-brainer. That is, it's unequivocally true. This principle is the foundation for the rest of this book. If you skip over this or don't get it right, you are likely to fail. It feels like the entire sales and marketing community argues for Principle I. So many salespeople makes rapid-fire calls without knowing specifically how they can help their prospects that sales leaders must feel obliged to make this argument.

Mike Weinberg, who wrote the great sales book, *New Sales. Simplified*, uses the acronym "USP" for "unique selling position." Your USP helps you gain a foothold in conversations with prospects on why they should buy from you. When you have a USP, you are approaching the prospect with specific content and intent. This is your foothold. Weinberg points out that if you cannot answer what your company can uniquely do, you are in trouble before you even start—meaning you have not done what you need to do in the prospecting phase, or even in the pre-prospecting phase. What is your company's USP? If you cannot answer this question, you have not fulfilled Principle 1. If you cannot answer this question, stop prospecting. Learn your USP before making another call.

In *This is Marketing,* Seth Godin encourages start-ups to stake out an unusual position in the market where less competition exists. If you and your company are a new vendor to your prospects, you will likely struggle if you try and compete for the piece of the pie that the incumbents securely hold. Don't go head-to-head with giants. Add value in a different, unique way. This requires you gain an understanding of who your competitors are and what they are doing well, as well as how your company is positioned to grow. Finding a unique or unusual use of your solution is a way of knowing specifically how your solution can help your customers. Do this, and you are meeting Principle 1. Do this and you are poised to succeed at creating and winning new sales in the enterprise.

In this foundational, pre-prospecting phase of building your business, understand the one big thing your company is best in the world at, rather than the many things your company may be able to do. As Jim Collins puts it in *Good to Great,* this is your company's "hedgehog concept." Undoubtedly, your company and you do many things well. You may be good at customer service, or response times, or your solutions may have features that are popular with your customers. Being good at these things is likely necessary for you to survive in the market. But what is it that your company is *great* at? What is the one thing your company does better than anyone else? Finding this will help you understand specifically how your company can help your prospects.

When I was new to large account prospecting, I quickly realized that my competitors had long, robust relationships with my biggest prospects. I was calling on accounts that had fifteen-year, twenty-year, or longer relationships with my competitors. These accounts and my competitors literally ate dinner together and had developed meaningful professional and personal relationships over long periods of time. How could a new guy like me make a call and swoop in to take that business? Assuming your solution is pretty much the same as your competitors, why would anyone consider listening to you?

Even in that environment of entrenched incumbents, I found that setting meetings was possible, but it was the wins that were highly difficult to achieve. Prospects were willing to meet with me because they found value identifying other solutions and trends in the market. This gave them the ability to claim that they had done their due diligence. The truth was, though, that they had no intention of changing solution providers. People build loyalty over time and are reluctant to interrupt those relationships. Moreover, people do not like change and if they feel something is working, they will avoid change. Fortunately, I did find an approach to help me compete.

The solution that worked for me was to find a niche. I found a very specific way that my solution could be undeniably helpful to my prospects. In *Mastering the Complex Sale,* Thull encourages us to understand business drivers. He states that "when working . . . in a highly competitive environment, establishing relevancy is crucial."[1] Indeed, I was not relevant to my prospects to a degree that would have them moving forward with my solution. I needed to establish relevancy amongst tried and true solutions and people. Finding a unique position is a great way to establish relevancy.

I discovered that an aspect of my solution was not commonly presented, but there was some demand. I leveraged this fact by calling on the small population of contacts that had that specific demand. These contacts were not accustomed to hearing from salespeople in my industry. I've also brought this concept to the same old prospects and it worked to keep me in the conversation. I knew very specifically how my product could help in a very specific manner, and with a specific population, and that may be the biggest reason for the successes that I have had in large account sales.

Before creating your own prospect list, you must know how your solution is unique and how those unique tools can help a specific segment of the population. I have children. I demand a robust camera in my phone because I want quality pictures of my children and I do not want to carry a separate camera. I chose my phone in large part because of the camera. The processing speed and memory capabilities and other features of what make my phone so expensive are necessary, and were prerequisites to the purchase, but I purchased my particular phone in large part for the camera. You have to find that same need in your own target market.

I have heard that people buy cars for the stereo and the cup holders. Could this be true? It seems ridiculous to me, but it may actually hold some truth. Check out https://www.thetruthaboutcars.com/2008/04/the-psychology-of-cupholders/. If I sold cars, I might take this into account. I might ask myself, is there a population of people more prone to purchasing a car because of the stereo or cup holders? Are there people who drink certain types of beverages, use particular drinking vessels or people who listen to certain types of music which require certain features in a stereo? How will answers to these questions help me sell a car? What are the cameras, cup holders and stereos of your solution?

When you are new to a company, in a sales role, you are generally put through extensive training on the products and how to present them. It is important that you absorb and retain this information. Be sure to ask lots of questions. Look at case studies. Read use cases. Understand as much as you can about what your solution does and does not do. Then do a side by side comparison with your competitors' solutions. If you are being promoted from small accounts to large accounts at the same company, you already know these capabilities, but you can now learn about how your solution resonates with large accounts.

Organize your information. Create a list of concrete, measurable benefits your solution provides your customers. Some of this information will be all around you in your company's messaging. Look at power point presentations, case studies, and other marketing material your company has published. Look at your company's website. For your solution(s), your firm has likely taken the time and made the investment to create succinct messaging on how it brings value to your customers. Is there anything in that messaging that can be a unique or unusual selling position—a hedgehog concept?

Another great resource for this data is previous transactions and current customers. You may have firsthand experience with organizations who have told you exactly how your solution helped them. Or you may have crafted a solution while working closely with a customer and seen how your solution helped that customer in a very specific way. If you are new to the company or if you do not have a story like this, talk to some of your peers and gather their stories. Stories are valuable—people gravitate to and retain stories over facts. What aspects of your solution are in these stories that are specific and unusual in your market? Can you retell that story to a small section of the market, in order to help them see how you can help their business?

If you have the time and resources, gather some of this information directly from your customer base. This is a fantastic exercise. There are many ways to do this, but some of the most common include conducting a survey to all or part of your customer base, or reaching out to your company's salespeople and having them ask their customers to provide a statement on where they have found value in your solution. If applicable, go back to customers you have worked with in the past and ask them to tell you what is working for them.

Know specifically how your solution helps people and companies. Gather all the details and historical evidence you can. The more you know and the more facts you have the better. This knowledge and these resources will be an enormous help in your account selection and prospecting, and will guide your sales. Once you have those stories, look for the specks of treasure in them.

PRINCIPLE 2: YOUR PROSPECT LIST SHOULD BE DIVERSE

We need to balance our win frequency with win size. You want to win the right number of accounts, as well as the right size accounts, and you want prospects that contain some diversity of character.

Your target list should have different size accounts by employee count, annual spend on your solution, or revenue. In your industry, you likely have two to ten main players—the very largest prospects. Winning one of those accounts would be epic and that single win alone could get you to your quota for the year, but the odds of winning one of those accounts each year are not great. If you get an opportunity with one, you could work on it for years only to have it fall apart in the end. Conversely, if you only focus on the smallest of your prospects, your total sales will fall short. The natural size of companies in your industry will lead your size makeup, and your account size makeup should be a pyramid, with the largest targets being the fewest on top and the smallest targets being the most on the bottom. We will walk through an example of what a breakdown looks like in the next principle.

You should also create prospect diversity by selecting prospects that represent different characteristics outlined below. The world is ever-changing. Your company is as well and so are you. Don't bank on a limited conception of your perfect customer. Some prospect characteristics, in which to leverage diversity, are:

- Industry
- Implementation timeframe
- Decision making structure
- Competitive incumbent situation
- Buyers that are in your sweet spot
- Buyers that challenge your company to deliver more cutting-edge solutions.

Diversity in your prospect list is going to help you get more timely wins, as well as keep you intellectually stimulated and contributing to the company for which you work. You can probably come up with some other ways to add diversity to your prospect list.

PRINCIPLE 3: PROSPECTS SHOULD SHARE TRAITS

Your prospect list should have diversity so that you create a balanced opportunity funnel. Your prospect list should also share some calculated, common traits. When diversity and likeness are planned and intentional, you are on your way to achieving the desired outcome of winning more business, more efficiently. Some themes that your accounts might share include industry, region and business challenges.

Prospect Traits:

Industry

Targeting a specific industry seems to be the first and most commonly practiced way to organize and distribute prospects amongst sales teams. Industries may have limited use of your solution and, no doubt, your company will have some type of focus around the industries on which you call. Not to be a downer, but some industries take many years to establish relationships of the length and depth that your competitors have. So don't be disappointed when one of your competitors has a twenty-year relationship with your prospect. Not only can you still overtake the incumbent, but now is the time to introduce yourself and begin your own relationship. Aside from investing time in industry relationships, you may focus on an industry to learn dialect and adapt to that culture.

Region

If not the first, region is probably the second most common way to organize and assign prospects. Staying within a given geographic area has obvious logistical benefits and if you are given free run of the country or globe, you should still look for prospect concentrations. Industries often clump naturally in given geographies. For example, technology is in Silicon Valley, manufacturing is in the Great Lakes, agriculture and energy are more in the Midwest, entertainment in Los Angeles, finance in Northeast Coast, etc. (Countless exceptions to these generalizations, I know). A regional focus will better enable you to set more appointments for the same trip—saving on time and money—and will help you establish credibility by letting prospects know that you have other prospects and customers in the same area.

Common Business Challenges and Needs

You can find common business needs or challenges and gather your prospects around those themes. Businesses have all kinds of challenges and no doubt your solutions help with some of those challenges. There are too many business challenges to list, but here are a few examples:

- Reduce labor costs
- Reduce the amount of time it takes to review data
- Increase available capital
- Increase workflow efficiency
- Reduce spend of a given solution

You should become an expert on what those challenges and needs are by following industry publications, learning from your peers, managers, and competitors, and undertaking general research on your own. The more you understand the challenges in your market(s), the better you can understand how your solution fixes them and how your solution needs to evolve to better fix those challenges. Become an expert in fixing a problem or set of problems and gather a list of prospects that appear to need your expertise.

Let's walk through a hypothetical example of an enterprise account executive (AE) that creates a list of prospects using Principles 1, 2, and 3. This AE's name is John and John is tasked with creating new customers in his territory—which is a three-state territory, comprised of small to mid-market economies. John has also been given a revenue goal for the year and John is aware of his team's average transaction size. Aside from his assigned territory, John has freedom to choose his prospects. John has the additional resource of existing prospects in his company's customer relationship management tool (CRM) from which to pull. John starts his prospect list with the data points he wants to include.

- Challenge(s) I can fix
- Employee count
- Industry

John works in a very competitive industry and, from his experience in the role from which he was promoted in SMB sales, John has a plan to set himself apart from the competition by solving a common need. Most companies leverage an enterprise resource planning (ERP) tool to track supply chain manufacturing and distribution. John has figured out that the human resources tools in his companies' solution have superior features that reduce the amount of HR staff needed. Rather than calling on operations management and IT—the most common contacts for his solution—John is going to get his foot in the door of his prospect accounts by calling on human resources management.

In *Target Opportunity Selling,* Nicholas Read states that "stars [successful sales/business development (BD) executives] begin by focusing on a business driver or trigger they know the customer has."[2] Before picking up the phone, John is creating a list of prospects for whom he believes he can solve a problem. Now for the easy part—creating a list of prospects strategically similar and yet diverse.

John feels comfortable with two industries—manufacturing and finance—so he starts there. Limiting his prospects to just two industries of focus allows John some submersion in both industries, while giving him plenty of diversity. Because he limits his reach, he will spend more time learning about and meeting people in each industry—which will yield some degree of expertise. One of the cities in his territory has a high concentration of the largest manufacturing targets. John will travel to that city regularly and it will be efficient to call on multiple prospects for the same trip. As he builds an opportunity funnel, John will visit prospects and customers—all in the same day.

Diversification has its advantages as well. If one industry slumps, his sales will take a limited hit. He is likely to stay more intellectually interested in day-to-day research. His solution is leveraged differently in finance and his company is eager to gain a bigger foothold in the finance industry. If John can gain key customers there, his company will have the additional benefits of growing their solution in a target industry. Spearheading that growth would be great for John's career.

Finally, John adds prospect size diversity when building his list of prospects. He selects ten accounts with over 1,000 employees, twenty accounts with 250 – 500 employees, and fifty accounts with 500 – 1,000 employees. He knows that onboarding just one company with over 1,000 employees will get him to his annual goal, but he is not betting on that single win. He would rather increase his odds of meeting his quota by working with smaller, medium, and large targets all at the same time.

John has a solid foundation of prospects because he starts with a problem that his solution can solve and John's prospect list is diverse, while maintaining related qualities. Before picking up the phone, John is ahead of the game with a unique concept to introduce to his prospects and a list that will get him more responses, yield a higher percentage of opportunities, maximize his time, and keep him engaged.

PRINCIPLE 4: BE EAGER TO DISQUALIFY YOUR PROSPECTS

I'm not good at this. I am an optimist and I enjoy getting creative in order to solve problems. But if I could have all the time back that I spent on opportunities with prospects that should have been disqualified, I would use that time in much better ways. I wish I had more "walk away power," as mentioned in the Ziglar Show podcast 788—more self-control to walk away from both prospects and opportunities that are not going to produce worthwhile sales.

I was once referred to a gentleman who owned a very small company and understood my product and how it could help him. This referral came from management, which was motivating. He embraced the nuances of my solution to an extent that an implementation would have been a sophisticated demonstration of my company's capabilities. I could not resist taking calls with him and even meeting him in person. Our meetings were intellectually fun for me. I consulted with him on how my company could help his business by leveraging my company's most cutting-edge capabilities. The problem was, when it came time to actually do business, there was no real volume of business to be had. His company's reach and wallet were not large enough to leverage my company's solution. After a two-hour, in-person meeting, several hours of phone calls and all the time I spent designing the solution on paper and in my mind, I finally disqualified the opportunity. I knew the potential was not there because the account was too small. I should have admitted this right away.

When you continue to call into an account that should not be on your list, the worst thing that can happen is that you *will* create an opportunity! But it will be a bad one. Think about that. The point of your outreach is to meet the right people and to present your solution, in order to sell that solution. Getting that process going with a bad prospect is a bad thing because you will waist your invaluable time and potentially more personal and company resources. Don't call on bad prospects because they might answer.

A bad prospect is one that will not or cannot adopt your solution at all or at the scale that you are after. So why would anyone go after a bad prospect? If you are not already familiar with this temptation, you will get to know it in large account sales. The temptations to go after bad prospects are daily and limitless. At least this has been my experience.

Bad Prospects

Here are some examples of bad prospects:

- *Too small* – The prospect is way too small but was referred to you and just wants to take up all your time to discuss this extremely small engagement. If you are in large account sales, you should ask someone on the SMB team if they want this account. Do not work on it yourself.
- *Solid "no"* – The decision makers at the prospect account have told you and your company "no" a hundred times. They have good reasons for this. They have a wonderful relationship with the incumbents and have no need for change. You cannot find a challenge of theirs that your solution can fix. It's very clear that it would take a miracle for you to make any real progress.

You might keep your eye on them and if there is material change with them or the incumbents, then that may be a good time to call. You might even check in once a year. But if the barriers are that high now, don't use your time on them.

- *Poor fit* – The prospect is nearly a good prospect but there is a major hitch that should lead you to disqualifying them. Since you are in contact with the right people and everything else is perfect—you spend hours trying to figure out a way to make it work. If there is a major reason why they prospect is not a good fit, you need to move on.

Be willing and even eager to disqualify prospects. There may be something to the idea of practicing presentation skills, messaging, and solution creation—at least early in your career. Generally, though, only call on accounts that are a strong candidate for your solution. Otherwise, you will waste time working on opportunities that do not get you to your goals.

Principles 1 – 4 are the first foundations of prospecting to large accounts. You must first thoroughly know how your solution can meet the needs of potential customers in the market. This is an ever-evolving knowledge because markets and solutions change. When you create or prioritize your prospect list, include diversity and commonalities, in order to build robust opportunity funnels, keep your interest level high, build industry expertise, and operate efficiently. Finally, what you don't do in large account sales may be almost as important as what you do. It's important that you spend your time wisely and pursue prospects that show the most promise while disqualifying any bad prospects.

CHAPTER TWO:
KNOW YOUR PROSPECTS

In this chapter, we will discuss the importance of knowing your prospects, different ways of knowing them, and discuss some ideas on how to manage and organize this information.

The principle we cover in this chapter is:

* Know your prospects in depth

In *The 48 Laws of Power*, there is a story about an art seller who targets large buyers. He essentially stalks them and gets to know everything about them from their habits to their personal interests. He gets to know the people who work for them. He studies them for a year or more before ever even approaching the buyer. When he finally does approach the buyer, he is able to present his product in a way that seems so incredibly serendipitous and tailored to the buyer that the buyer could never say no; furthermore, the buyer would never buy from anyone else after meeting this seemingly perfect seller.

The two most common ways of assigning prospects are by territory and by industry. In either case, even if you are on an organized
team, you likely have ten or fewer major prospects. You should be
stalking these major prospects frequently. If you are fortunate enough
to spend years or even your entire career in a single industry, as many
enterprise account executives do, your depth of knowledge about the
major prospects will be extensive indeed. The longer you stay close to an
industry, the more nuanced, relevant, and interesting your knowledge
of key prospects in that industry becomes. Of course, you likely are
developing contacts and relationships along the way. This depth of
knowledge and these relationships hold an immense amount of value
for companies who employ salespeople. You become a true expert
with rarified knowledge, which you will no doubt capitalize on in
promotions and compensation.

PRINCIPLE 5: KNOW YOUR PROSPECTS IN DEPTH

You cannot know too much about your prospects, but the depth of
your information gathering for each account depends on the number
of prospects that you have. I have met salespeople who have only
one account. They are responsible for knowing that account at a very
intimate level. They know about events, significant news, small news,
management changes, other personnel changes, new products, and
generally as much as possible about that one account. When you only
have one or only a few accounts, it is your responsibility to be the expert
for your company on that customer or prospect. All that knowledge
will assist in your company's bottom line and your sale.

Organize Prospect Data

You should be using a CRM and a spreadsheet to gather and save
this information. This information is gold so please take very good care

of it—save it in multiple formats and back it up regularly. It's true it is tedious—I don't like keeping multiple records, like a CRM *and* a spreadsheet—but you need to do this for a couple reasons. One, your company has likely invested in a CRM and needs you to use it. So use it. Other people in your company likely need access to your data. You also need your own record of this extremely valuable information and it's great to have it in an additional format that you can customize anyway. A spreadsheet is useful for this purpose. Back this information up daily to your hard drive *and* to a cloud drive.

Your data fields may include the following, and you will likely personalize this list with points relevant to your solution. These fields are likely in smaller spreadsheet fields, so keep them very brief. Here are some data fields you might use to build and organize prospect information.

- *Personal, professional and transactional history* – This includes the people at your prospect account who you know, connections shared between current colleagues and prospect contacts, and any business the company you work for and your prospect account have completed.
- *Solution* – Just a few words on the core of what your prospect produces or provides.
- *Why they are a top prospect* – A quick summery of why this account has made your list. A couple examples are "worked with SVP at last company," "CFO background in [my solution]," "my CEO connected with their management team."
- *Geography* – List their HQ and other relevant geographical information.
- *Size indicators* – I like to use employee count because it's quick and easy to find on LinkedIn. More exact information is better if you have it. If you can find more detailed information like annual revenue in your territory, total revenue, or annual

spend on your solution, that's even better. Sources for these numbers may come from industry groups and information services companies, like Lexis Nexis and Wolters Kluwer.

- *Win strategy* – This is different from a long form account plan. This is a quick, nutshell statement. Some examples are "leverage previous sales in NY office," "cold call HR team," "follow up with John Doe at trade show."
- *Key People* – We will cover contact selection at length in a later chapter. Here you list one or a few of those contacts.
- *Events* – These include your prospect's summits or annual show in which customers, select employees and vendors are invited. List here trade shows and other industry events where your prospect will attend.
- *Incumbents* – Incumbents are your competitors who own or are already doing business with your prospect. I find this to be highly valuable information and is often protected by your prospect. If they share with you who the incumbent is, that is a win. The fact that they shared this with you is a good sign that you are making progress.
- *New products, services, and solution changes* – This is one of the most valuable pieces of information to have when cold calling. When you call your prospect and cite that they just made a big change or released a new product or service, your prospect will be impressed. This will set you apart from other people calling on this account. We will cover leveraging this information to create opportunities in depth in Section Two.
- *Company culture* – Challenge yourself to capture your prospect's culture in a few words. If you and your team's culture clashes with your prospect's culture, disaster awaits. You need to keep your eye on who they are, in reality as well as in the public image they try to present. Examples include "sharp

dress, multiple non-profits," "flat hierarchy," "embrace integration partners."

- *Goals* – Understanding your prospect's challenges and initiatives is central to prospecting and opportunity planning. You will find these in mission statements, conversations with their employees, through word of mouth, and during earnings calls.
- *Media* – Do they broadcast? Where and what do they share? Does their CEO take to Twitter? Answers to these questions will give you insights into your prospect's culture and valuable prospecting information.
- *Notes* – I like to keep a large field for general notes. Put anything here from noteworthy contact information to frustration or excitement with the prospecting efforts.

Updating this information could become a full-time job by itself, and it is a big part of your job. If I had to put an ideal percentage of time you should spend on building and keeping up this information, I might say 10 – 50 percent of your time. Large account sales is largely about what and who you know, so commit the time to keeping this information up to date.

There are a few ways you can keep up with this information efficiently. Follow your prospects on every social media platform they or their company uses, subscribe to industry publications, set up Google alerts, and subscribe to your prospect's email campaigns. You can sign up for LinkedIn job alerts to track management changes. These streams of information allow you to passively scan for important updates from your prospects and get to know them in more depth.

You likely will have more than one prospect and customer and, unlike the art dealer in *The 48 Laws of Power*, you probably cannot know everything about multiple prospects. You should, however, know as much as you can about your prospect companies with the time that you have. Let's now discuss getting to know your contacts at the companies in which you are prospecting.

CHAPTER THREE: CONTACT SELECTION PRINCIPLES

n this chapter, we will cover three principles of choosing contacts. These principles are:

- Start at the Top
- Do Background Research when Selecting Contacts
- Find Multiple Contacts

You are prospecting to people. People are nuanced, unpredictable, complex, and ever-changing. Your contacts have a role and no doubt they will fulfil their assignments within the scope of purchasing your solution, but they will do it in their own way. When choosing contacts, consider and plan to approach your contacts as the individuals they are, while respecting traditional decisioning hierarchies.

PRINCIPLE SIX: START AT THE TOP

You have probably experienced a situation where you were working with a person or people only to find out they are not the one(s) making the buying decision. It's frustrating, right? Did your solution's message get diluted? Did it get entirely misrepresented? Of course, you're not able to get direct feedback in those situations—that feedback is being relayed through the filter that is your contact.

You want to be as close to the final decision maker or decision makers as possible and that is often possible! In *Selling to the C-Suite,* Read and Bistritz share some great ideas on how to access the C-Suite—work through referrals, send a letter or email prior to a cold call, and find a sponsor that can get you access to the C-Suite. We will cover how to approach executives in more depth in Section Two, but for now believe me that you can and will gain access to executives at your largest accounts.

Select contacts at your target accounts that are at the highest points of decision making. If you talk to an executive who generally has no hand in decision making with your solution, you may bring to light a problem or opportunity which that person cares about. This, of course, can be a big win for you. When your champion is an executive or has a large amount of direct reports, her introductions and direction will be a boon for you.

If you are selling through a channel, there may be solutions that allow you to start anywhere in the organization, such as solutions that are not part of a single, large purchase. If yours is a "bolt-on"—an add-on to a solution—you may be able to work with any salespeople at your prospect account. This is common in software and finance. In this case, it may be your goal to have a programmatic relationship with the core product seller, in which they add your solution to all their proposals. Until you get to that point, you could start working with contacts at any level in the hierarchy and work your way up. This is the "foot-in-the-door" technique, which can also be leveraged with siloed enterprises, in which you have multiple buyers in different departments or geographies, but you have not yet won the account wholesale. This technique does not start at the top and is not as ideal. Use it only when you have exhausted working directly with Senior Management.

PRINCIPLE 7: DO BACKGROUND RESEARCH WHEN SELECTING CONTACTS.

You want to uncover aspects of your contact's background, current role, and connections that give you and your solution an edge. Knowing your contacts will help you pair yourself with people in your target accounts with which you have the highest odds for success. In *Influence,* Cialdini asserts that people *want* to say yes to people they like.He uses the Tupperware party as an example of a sales channel based on the natural phenomenon that people buy from those they know and like. So when selecting contacts to call on in your prospect accounts, choose people who are most likely to like *you*—people with similar hobbies, connections, backgrounds interests, and values.

You are trying to uncover their preferences, biases, expertise, what they are comfortable with, and what they dislike or want to avoid. Thull calls this "creative profiling" and suggests that you should identify the "optimum point of entry"in vetting your contacts. Here is what to look for:

- *Time in current role* – I like to call on contacts who are new to their role. When a person starts a new role, they are less set in their ways and are in the process of developing their approach. Somebody who has been in their role for less than a year is more likely to adopt a new way of doing things than somebody who has been in their role for ten or twenty years. That new way of doing things can include your solution.

- *Time at company* – Although I have had success working with people new to a company, I prefer to call on people who have been at the company for a longer period. They are going to know more people, how decisions get made, and know other historically relevant information that will help you.

    Perhaps an ideal contact is someone new to a role but who has tenure at the company.

- *Work history* – When selecting a contact to call on, choose those who give you an advantage. Something I always look for is a contact that is biased toward the nature of my solution. You can uncover those biases in a contact's work history by discovering their track record of working with your solution or your type of solution.

    You may also find some quirky information here that may help you later, like the contact's historical duration at companies, volunteer information, and background in other roles and with other companies.

- *Alignment with professional organizations historically and today* – LinkedIn will show you organizations that your prospect is a member of or part of. LinkedIn also shows other roles, such as involvement in nonprofits. Learning that your prospect is a member of professional communities and organizations will help you to understand how their time is spent, their motivations, and how you may call on them.

- *Shared Contacts* – Leveraging existing relationships is an acquired skill. You can call on a contact until you're blue in the face and if they don't know you, you may never reach them. Some people are less responsive to cold calls. An introduction from a quality, shared contact, often becomes an instantaneous, meaningful connection.

LinkedIn makes finding these relationships easier to investigate with their first, second, and third-degree connections feature. I also like to keep records of contacts that I have worked well with in a spreadsheet, along with any connections they have to my target accounts.

- *Education background and geographical history* – This is information that can help you make more personal connections with your prospects. People often take pride in their alma mater as well as places they are from and places they like. I have seen connections made over the telephone very quickly when people can share stories and talk about locations that resonate emotionally.

- *Hobbies and other personal interests* – Sales 101 demands that you start a meeting with rapport around something personal. You are trained to walk into an office and look at trophies and pictures and other memorabilia that allow you to start a personal conversation. I do not think this is a waste of your time or your prospect's time. I acknowledge that (in large ticket sales, at least) people buy from people and it's important to relate to your contacts as the unique people that they are. Rapport of this kind is more important in enterprise and SMB sales because you are likely to have a longer relationship with the buyer in enterprise sales than you do in transactional SMB sales.

Let's walk through an example of how you might use these data points to your advantage in selecting a contact to call on. You are selling a software-as-a-service product and you are selecting contacts at your prospect account. You know you need to talk to the Director of IT. You also see that they have a Vice President of Infrastructure and a Vice President of Operations, and your solution lends itself to working with any one or all three of these titles.

Look at the Director of IT on LinkedIn. Look at her work history. You see that she has been in her role for just three months. This represents opportunity. You add her as a contact. Now look through the work history of the Vice President of Infrastructure. You see that he used to work for a software developer that only sells licensed software. This could be a red flag because he may have philosophical differences with the nature of your product. You also note that he lived in your home state for ten years and he is a member of a professional organization that you just joined. Add him to your list but with caution. The Vice President of Operations has no contacts in common with you and her work history does not point to any direct involvement with IT, software, or SaaS. Although you may run into her in the sales process, do not add her to your list to call on.

Do background research when selecting contacts in order to maximize the odds that you will create an opportunity and win that opportunity. You will get stuck working with people you did not select, and they are sometimes averse to your solution because they are threatened, do not benefit to a large enough degree, or simply disagree with your approach. Knowing your contacts, however, will help you navigate your working relationship with these people and give you direction on who you pull into the project.

PRINCIPLE 8: FIND MULTIPLE CONTACTS

This one will be contentious with some of you, and second nature to others. One of the unwritten rules of working a sales opportunity is to not go over or around your sponsor. I think this is a good rule of thumb, but what we are talking about here is *prospecting* large accounts, not working through an opportunity. It makes sense to develop multiple contacts early in the prospecting phase, while you are not yet limited by the prospect on who you can work with.

Your First Contact May Be Key in Helping Your Prospecting

In *Selling to the C-Suite,* we see that the two most likely ways C-level executives take a sales meeting are from a recommendation from someone in their company, or in the form of referral of someone outside their company. You are often prospecting to people who will get you the meeting with the C-level executive. You may not be successful in getting the meeting directly with C-level executives, but you may get the ear of someone who can get you that meeting. So, know the executives, but also know the contacts around them.

Multiple Contacts Will Be Part of Your Sale

According to challengerinc.com—the online resource from the creators of *The Challenger Sale*—the average size of a buying group has increased from 5.2 in 2014 to as high as 10.2 in 2018.[3] I can't think of a single transaction in my commercial sales career where there was a decision maker acting alone in a transaction. Even in SMB sales, an owner of a small company will consult with others before purchasing solutions of any value. A large ticket, complex sale in an enterprise will certainly involve multiple stakeholders. It only makes sense to list and call on multiple contacts at your prospect accounts. Often, these multiple stakeholders will represent different departments in the enterprise.

Research Different Departments

Discover multiple prospects that work in different areas, like Finance, HR, Sales, and IT. Aside from the fact that your solution likely impacts multiple business units, a good reason to discover contacts from different business units is that you will be able to simultaneously call on them without soliciting members of the same team. In our example of John calling on HR management in Chapter One, he will increase his odds of creating an opportunity if he also calls on IT and operations management. In *Mastering the Complex Sale,* Thull makes the point that it's a good idea to call on unconventional contacts not only because they have fewer barriers to entry, but also because they may be more affected by your solution than the usual suspects. I have often gotten to the table through the unconventional contact whose business will really benefit from my help.

Multiple Contacts Can Save the Deal

I have also benefited from working with multiple contacts during an opportunity crisis. When your sale is in limbo, it may be because your first contact is going a different direction from your solution. You can save the sale when you have additional champions to defend your solution. I once created an opportunity through a managing member of a sales organization named Sarah. Sarah and I had a nice rapport and she introduced me to her manager, Jim, who was also on board with my proposal. I worked closely with Sarah and Jim for several months making nice progress. Sarah then received a promotion and left for a different department. This was great for her and I was happy for her, but it changed the dynamic of our opportunity.

Jim assigned one of his team, Alexie, to the onboarding of my solution and this was when my sale got in trouble. Alexie—the person now in charge of my sale—had a completely different view of my solution and how it could benefit her and her company. It wasn't long before my original solution had changed in scope and in structure. My opportunity was in serious danger of being a fraction of quality and size than originally conceived. I worked with Alexie for well over a year and was forced to do things her way. As time went on, I had less access to Jim and my opportunity took the shape of Alexie's conception and not Sarah's, mine, or Jim's original vision of what my solution would look like in their ecosystem.

Fortunately, I developed relationships with influential people throughout this engagement because my opportunity would soon be challenged. I started the opportunity with a longer list of contacts than just Sarah and as the opportunity grew, I added to that list and eagerly developed rapport with influencers in other departments. One day, almost out of the blue, my solution was thrown out by Alexie and Jim. The reason was a philosophical difference between our two companies of the different ways to leverage my solution. Alexie's ideas had won out and taken root with Jim, but I was able to rely on a few of the new contacts to bring me back to the table. These new contacts were more aligned with my company on the best use of our solution and they were eager to provide their sponsorship because they believed my solution could help them.

In *Game-Changer,* David McAdams lists relationships as one of the six ways to change a game. McAdams' perspective is one of game-theory, which is a relevant and perhaps helpful platform for you to use, to win with your prospects. Your prospects are likely creating many of the rules on how you can engage, and you can play the game of winning their business—playing within their rules—by building and leveraging relationships.

At this point in your process, when you are just creating your contact list, do yourself a favor and identify contacts from which you will inevitably draw strength from during the long sales cycles inherent to enterprise sales. Multiple contacts can help you out of tough situations. They can also help you expand your solution's footprint at your target account.

WINS BEGET WINS

When selling and developing revenue-generating partnerships in the enterprise, success with one contact will lead to success with more contacts for the following reasons:

- *Trust* – People want a proven solution. Humans are more comfortable doing what has already been done. You won over your first sponsor and that should be the hardest win. That person can now vouch for your reliability and character. As you earn the trust of more contacts, those contacts will in turn vouch for you with even more contacts and the growth becomes exponential.

- *Use case* – I am always amazed at how difficult it can be to communicate the uses, details, and even benefits of a given solution. People are embedded in their own ways of thinking about the problems in front of them. When you bring a solution that represents an enhanced or a different way of addressing their problems, they sometimes just don't get it even though you are masterful in explaining how your solution can help them. They may need to see it in use at their company so they can relate to it and internalize how your solution will help them. When you have a model of how your solution has helped someone in a new organization, that real story is more powerful than your explanations, which are only concepts.

- *Politics* – If somebody else has it, I want it in order to not feel left out, less deserving, or less important. Contacts will demand access to your solution to prove that they deserve to have it and to leverage any tool that gives them an advantage.

- *The Network Effect* – In *This is Marketing,* Seth Godin explains that ideas spread through the "peer-to-peer movement of ideas"—not just via social media technology—but also through more grass roots means. An example he uses is someone wanting to organize a demonstration and trying to get people to the demonstration via a bus ride. The more people who come, the better for the demonstration, and they would have a better time on the bus ride. Your contact may need others to adopt your solution in order to get access to it at all or they may just have a better experience if others share the solution. So they may promote your idea for you. It often makes people's lives better when their peers adopt the same solution as the one they have adopted.

Select multiple contacts from the beginning and gather as many allies along the way as possible. This will get you into more doors and increase your odds of winning. Also, knowing people is good for your career. As your contacts move to other companies, they can bring your solution into those new companies making your job easier.

Large companies are their own universes comprised of people who are also each their own complex system of biases, preferences, fears, and aspirations. Consider leveraging the principles in Chapter Three to increase your odds of entry into your target accounts and of successful positioning of your solution.

This concludes Section One. We have worked through principles of preparation. We discussed choosing your targets, knowing your prospects, and choosing your contacts. I have spent way, way too much time calling on the wrong accounts and my hope is that you will embrace some of these principles, so that you spend less time making the same mistakes I have. Let's transition now to discussing principles of outreach into these accounts, which you have now so carefully vetted.

SECTION TWO: PROSPECTING METHODS

Where does all that time go in large account sales? What are people doing if they're not making calls all day? Are the techniques of prospecting to large accounts different from the techniques of prospecting in SMB sales? Is there any point in cold calling executives at Fortune 500 companies? These are some of the questions I had when I was new to large account sales. In Section Two, we will explore where and how you are spending your time and the techniques of prospecting to large accounts.

If you are in large account sales, you likely had success in SMB sales, and therefore you have some grasp on how to manage yourself for the demands of sales. In Section Two, we will cover time management strategies for effective prospecting in large account sales. You likely are already doing some of these, but hopefully you will find some new tricks as we work through Chapter Four, and it may also further reinforce what you are already doing well.

In this section, I'm going to suggest that you do less prospecting in large account sales, than you did in SMB sales. Not only is too much prospecting now a poor use of your time, but by making too many calls you can also damage your reputation with your prospects and in your long-term career. We will work through the little wins that come in large account prospecting, discuss the importance of each and every call, and talk about creating and cultivating relationships that last many years.

You will have fewer prospects and every interaction you have with them now carries more weight, so we will discuss the importance of customizing every solicitation. Never call a prospect just to check a box and get another dial in. *Always* have a reason to call. The reason you are calling will be custom for each prospect. In Chapter Six, we will go through ideas on why you might call your prospect other than the obvious, "Hey, do you want to buy what I am selling?"

As Section Two wraps up, we will work through forms of prospecting that you can use in large account sales. Chapter Seven will cover ways to use your phone, use written messaging, and how to prospect in person. You are likely a proficient communicator in all these modes of prospecting, and I hope that you will pick up some new tricks for using these modes of prospecting specifically for large account sales.

CHAPTER FOUR: MANAGING YOURSELF FOR EFFECTIVE PROSPECTING

In this chapter, you will learn some ways to manage your time and energy in order to meet your prospecting objectives. We will cover the principle of prioritization:

- Prioritize Prospecting Above All Else

What motivates you? It's important to know the answer to this question so you can use the right motivation to propel yourself through less-than-fun tasks, like prospecting. Whatever your motivation is, I suggest you manage yourself, or focus on selecting the right habits and monitoring them, in order to be effective—sounds obvious, but it's not. Professionals who do not manage themselves toward conscious results (goals) too often spend their priceless time achieving things other than their assigned and self-imposed goals.

Manage yourself for effectiveness. Effectiveness in your role is very likely quota attainment. If you are in sales, that number may consist of multiple factors like profitability and your quota certainly contains a total sales number. You should manage yourself to hit that number. If you are in business development, your number may be more dynamic, but you surely have expectations you need to meet. You should manage yourself to meet those expectations.

According to Peter Drucker, as put forth in *The Effective Executive,* effectiveness can be learned. In his view, being effective is not the result of character traits, personality, or values. Rather, "effectiveness is a habit." Or, we might call effectiveness a group of habits. Here are those habits, according to Mr. Drucker:

- Know where your time goes
- Focus on outward contribution
- Build on strengths, not weaknesses
- Concentrate on a few areas that will produce results
- Make effective decisions[4]

This chapter will focus on habits one and four.

You doubtless have many demands on your time—both personal and from the company for which you work. Some of those demands are not negotiable and are unavoidable. If your manager puts a meeting on your calendar, you probably cannot get away with declining that meeting. If you have an emergency with a very important customer, you should probably drop everything and address that emergency. If your manager gives you a timebound task with short notice, that will disrupt your schedule as well. Or your child fell sick at school and needs to be picked up . . . I acknowledge that there are going to be demands on your time that are out of your control.

In 2020 and potentially into the future, many of us work from a home office and time management skills are more important than ever. Distractions and temptations toward personal activities abound in your home. You may be tempted to enjoy the luxuries of your home during work hours. You may be distracted toward those things you normally do at home like taking in shows, resting, and visiting with friends and neighbors.

In our connected times, distractions and information are more than plentiful. The very place where your work—your computer workstation—has enough information, entertainment, and social platforms to hold your attention indefinitely. The challenge is no longer how to access information and entertainment. The challenge now is limiting content from your mindshare. Through all of this, focus on Peter Drucker's habits one and four. Track and manage your time in order to concentrate on the most important use of your time, which is prospecting.

PRINCIPLE 9: PRIORITIZE PROSPECTING ABOVE ALL ELSE

If you are going to be a consistent contributor, attain quota, and make great money, prospecting is the most important thing you can do with your time. Ensure that you make time to prospect. In sales, you need to make things happen. Your organization likely has some type of indirect channel, inbound lead system, and other business units which will yield new opportunities for you. These channels are never enough to get you to quota. Prospecting, albeit in different channels and via a variety of methods, is generally an Enterprise Sales Executive's primary channel for new opportunities. Prospecting yields many benefits, such as the below.

- *Opportunities that yield wins* – Your primary purpose for prospecting is to create opportunities. You need opportunities to convert a percentage of them into wins, which counts toward your quota and goals assigned to you. Opportunities are the essential building blocks to your success.

- *Opportunities that yield leverage* — When you have a full opportunity funnel:
  - » You have the leverage to prioritize opportunities that are better for your organization and your paycheck.
  - » You have more negotiating power with prospects.
  - » You are a more valuable employee. This is good for job security.
  - » You demonstrate you can execute. Your company will trust you with better accounts and leads.
  - » Your time is more valuable when you have a full opportunity funnel and so you will tend to call better prospects.

- *A bigger network* — As you call on prospects, you will develop professional relationships. Those relationships can lead to opportunities in the short term and down the road. That network represents a lot of value to hiring firms, especially if you stay in the same industry. That network can make your career.
- *Control over your career* — By picking up the phone and bringing in business, you create momentum toward success. You are making good things happen. As you accumulate wins, you are building a track record that becomes your career.
- *Control over your income* — Many salespeople are content with their base pay and benefits. These people are only trying to make quota to keep their job, but most sales jobs do not have a cap on commission income. I have seen several top salespeople become the highest paid people in the entire company! Sales can be very lucrative, and you can increase your income by increasing the number opportunities that you have. To get more opportunities and achieve elite levels of income, *prospect more*. What would you do with double the income you have now?

Schedule it

Put prospecting time on the calendar! To ensure it gets done, schedule it. Then schedule around it. Protect this time unless it's absolutely necessary to schedule over it or an emergency comes up in your day. Mike Weinberg states that "no one defaults to prospecting mode,"[5] meaning you don't just find yourself prospecting. You may find yourself looking at internet sites and social media, but you don't just find yourself doing the hard work of picking up the phone and calling a prospect. Weinberg's solution to this is "time blocking," which he refers to as making an appointment with yourself. Mange yourself to ensure execution of prospecting by scheduling prospecting on your calendar.

Now that you are making those calls, establish motivating goals for your prospecting. Establish daily, weekly, and even annual prospecting goals. If you come from small and medium business sales, then you are already familiar with "activity metrics" and you need very little review here. The concept of tracking your calls and emails in enterprise sales is the same, but your numbers are just far fewer. I still find value in tracking activity metrics in large account sales because it helps me with accountability. I suggest that you use activity metrics for the same reason.

Short, Focused Prospecting Intervals

Use short, focused time intervals for your prospecting. Using short time intervals will help ensure that you complete the prospecting session and they help us maintain focus and reduce interruptions. A business coach of mine suggested I keep my prospecting intervals short and referred to this as "The Pomodoro Technique." Francesco Cirillo published a book called *The Pomodoro Technique* which you may wish to read. The basic idea is that one can be more productive when using focused sessions of about twenty minutes to complete tasks. I like this approach for large account prospecting because you need to maintain awareness during your prospecting sessions. In SMB sales, you could get away with distracted prospecting. In large account prospecting, you need to be more alert due to the limited amount of opportunities and the importance of each contact.

Use short time intervals for prospecting because this approach works better in a home office. You are more likely working from home in large account sales. As I am writing this during COVID-19, we are mostly all working from home. SMB sales is more often a call center environment whereas large account sales is more often a remote, isolated environment. Of course, large account executives spend time in the corporate office, but they are frequently traveling and often work from a remote office a larger percentage of the time comparatively. Working from a home office has a different pace. Your time at your desk can be more productive because there is less interaction with coworkers.

There is a great Wall Street Journal article, "I've Worked from Home for 22 Years. Here is What I've Learned"[6] by Alexandra Samuel, that addresses working at home. Samuel states that the eight-hour workday is too long for the focused work of the home office. Since you are not spending time chatting with peers, you are working when at your desk; your time is condensed. Therefore, the same length of day in the corporate office should be longer than a day spent in your home office. As long as you keep those home distractions to before and after work, your home workday should be shorter. Samuel also points out that you need to have some type of time management system for the home office. Using something like the Pomodoro Technique and scheduling prospecting time in the calendar are time management systems that have worked for me.

Don't Stop

Keep your prospecting up even when you are busy with opportunities, other tasks demanded in your role, and personal matters. If you continue to prospect when you have a full opportunity funnel, you can create exponential success. This continually increasing success comes from creating opportunities, even when you have opportunities, and letting the weaker opportunities fall from your attention. The idea is that when you honor your daily prospecting time—no matter how busy you are—the people you call on, the accounts you call on, and the opportunities you are willing to engage in are of higher quality. Your time is more valuable and so you are pickier. When you are busy, you will not engage in wasteful tasks and so the quality of your engagements increases. As the quality of your work improves, you continue to prospect, and the quality of your opportunities and how you engage with them continues to improve. You are creating momentum in the right direction. This is a tough discipline and I struggle with it to this day, but I do my best with it and have collected dividends from keeping up prospecting even when busy. I hope that you will prospect even when you are successful and busy.

Prioritize prospecting above all else. You are taking control of your income and your career. It's too easy to neglect prospecting, so schedule it in your calendar. Protect that time. Break that time up in short, focused intervals—especially when working from a home office. When your opportunity funnel is full, keep prospecting! The longer you can maintain your prospecting schedule, the more successful you will be.

CHAPTER FIVE:
PROSPECTING CADENCE

n this chapter, we will look at how many calls to make and I will give you perhaps the most important principle of this book:

- Do Less Prospecting

My big evolution in enterprise sales came when I finally accepted that I needed to do less outreach than I had been doing in SMB sales. I learned that I should call less and use the time I saved to do the research discussed in Section One. My hope for you is that you will not spend all your time making short-sighted calls. For many coming out of SMB sales, making lots of calls is what they know and what they are good at—indeed, it is what is necessary to be successful in small account sales. That was me. I was good at picking up the phone and executing a lot of outreach. I was successful because I was willing to make a lot of calls. Making a large volume of calls is what I considered the hard work of sales. When I got promoted into enterprise sales, I wanted success more than ever and was willing to work hard for it. So, I kept on making a lot of calls.

One of my first assignments in enterprise sales was to attend a trade show and set meetings with a segment of the attendees. My first reaction—make fifty or more calls a day of course! I wanted to do a good job and making a lot of calls is the way to do that, right? More activity equals more opportunities equals more sales—this is what we were taught. I built my early sales career by keeping prospecting activity high. Turns out I made zero appointments with enterprise targets at that trade show. But I will say that I learned a lot about the attendees through this large amount of activity.

I tried to apply this approach, when reaching out to senior executives at large companies:

This is a linear approach, in which more calls lead to more meetings, which lead to more sales. If I made fifty calls a day and talked to five decision makers, set one meeting, and completed one sale, that would be fantastic! But I was calling on people who did not freely give their time and energy. I needed to add value from the first moment I engaged the prospect. In order to create that value, I needed to understand my company's unique capabilities and the prospect's specific needs. It takes time to create that value, and that time comes out of time that you previously spent making calls. This is more of an integrated, cyclical process, which is constantly changing as our prospect's needs change.

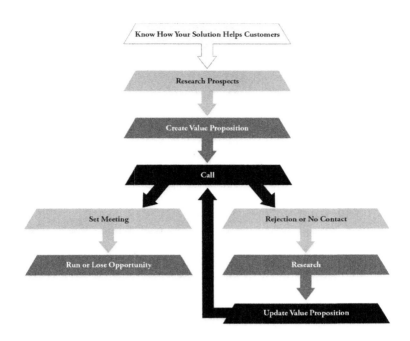

The biggest reason why I wrote this book was to share the lessons I learned from the crisis that I experienced around activity metrics. I would go on to spend the first part of my enterprise sales career trying to achieve success by making too many calls. If you take one thing from this book, take the fact that making too many calls is not only a poor use of time, but can be destructive to your short-term goals as well as your career.

PRINCIPLE 10: DO LESS OUTREACH THAN WHAT YOU DID IN SMB SALES

You are now in an environment where the quality of your interaction will be a larger determination of your success than the quantity of your interaction. Simply making the call is no longer the largest determining factor for success, like it was in SMB sales. You absolutely need to pick up the phone—just less often.

More calls do not equal more sales

In *Managing Major Sales*, Neil Rackham and Richard Ruff question the commonly assumed principle that more calls equal more sales. They acknowledge that examples showing increased sales resulting from increased call volume are common, and that these examples are in small ticket sales. "Major account sales are large, multicall [sic], and almost invariably more dependent on skill and strategy than on energy and enthusiasm."[7] They add that focusing on call volume leads to:

- A focus on small sales
- A proliferation of paperwork and administration
- Attention to the wrong end of the sales pipeline
- Demotivation of top salespeople[8]

If most of your focus is on call volume, as it rightly was in SMB sales, you are likely going to get these adverse results.

Jill Konrath states that "targeting: it's not a numbers game," and speaks to how tempting it can be to call everyone.[9] She makes the statement that selling is "no longer about spending hours on the phone calling hundreds of people hoping to find someone who will meet with you."[10] When you were in SMB sales and had a very general product that works great for a very general population, volume prospecting of this sort probably worked. Not so in Enterprise sales.

You have fewer prospects so why would you do the same amount of prospecting? Let's say you have fifty prospects and five contacts at each prospect account. That's 250 prospects. If you work five days a week and make fifty calls a day, are you going to call all your contacts every week? Probably not. In SMB sales you likely had thousands of contacts you were calling on. You could make calls all day every day and not call the same contact more than once a month or even once a quarter. Even if you did have a much larger prospect list, though, you would not want to use all your time making calls.

In major account sales, a large amount of your time is used in research and strategy, whereas in SMB sales most of your time is used making calls. I have seen SMB sales teams that discourage and even banned sales representatives from researching their prospects before calling. These prospects had already been vetted and sales management's strategy is to make a lot of calls into these already qualified prospects. This approach is appropriate in that environment. You, however, are calling into select accounts and *each call matters*. If each call matters, you need to know as much as possible about the prospect and the contact in the industry in order to deliver the right message at the right time. We will cover this in depth with Principle 11.

I am going to give you some suggestions on call volume. These are far from prescriptive and are only meant to give you a general idea of the call volume which takes place in major account sales. In my work history and in observation of my peers throughout my career, I would guess that an average number of prospects is one hundred (this is a nice round number as well), with five to ten contacts per prospect account, and I would guess an average number of prospecting calls per week, for the average enterprise sales executive, is about twenty. I have made as many as a hundred calls per week and I have known major account salespeople who almost never make a call and can rely solely on email. You make more calls when you're building a pipeline and may make fewer calls when you have a full opportunity funnel. So, in the end, twenty calls a week is a viable number to consider. You are likely making one to four calls per hour. It may take fifteen minutes to research your history with the prospect, check for any news, call and message a contact—and that's if you are very familiar with the prospect and account. You should do this research before almost every call (unless you just called them a couple days before and are following up on that call). So, four calls an hour is a lot.

You are making fewer calls and it is harder to set meetings, so there are fewer positive results compared to that which you are accustomed. Aside from setting meetings, there are other positive and important outcomes to your large account prospecting. In large account sales and business development, you must gather lots of other, smaller wins that end up resulting in the larger win. Again, this is a cyclical engagement, rather than linear. The little wins are bits of information you get that allow you to create a better value proposition and approach with the prospect.

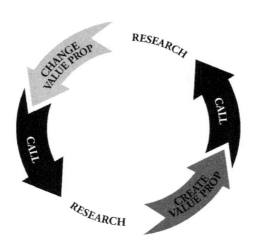

THE LITTLE WINS

In enterprise sales prospecting, a win is not just creating an opportunity or even setting an appointment but includes helpful outcomes that contribute to your overall mission. I can count the number of times on one hand that I made a first call to an enterprise prospect and created a solid opportunity. I have made calls for weeks and never reached a decision influencer or decision maker. This is in stark contrast to the first sales job I had out of college where I would schedule a good five appointments per day in only a couple hours of calling. But there are other positive outcomes when prospecting to select accounts. Positive outcomes from prospecting into select accounts include the following:

- *Gain Knowledge* – If I pick up the phone and learn something about a prospect's company, product, or personnel that I did not already know—that's a win. This is particularly true if this is information that you cannot find in research. If I learned something about the industry I'm prospecting into—that's a win.

- *Meet someone at the prospect company and build rapport* – Principle 6 requires that you start with contacts higher in seniority. You may also benefit from just talking with other people at the company who you suspect are not involved in the decision to onboard your solution. You can talk with anyone who answers the phone, people in different departments and particularly people at trade shows to learn information that is not available in your prospect's published resources. If you build enough of a relationship with someone like this, you can even go back for information or advice that you otherwise could not get.

- *Disqualify a prospect* – Principle 4 requires that you are eager to disqualify prospects. You will frequently come across information in your prospecting that helps you to disqualify your prospects. This is a win because it clears your prospect list of the bad prospects and allows you to focus your time on productive prospects.

- *Disqualify a contact* – This is a great outcome because you can stop wasting your time. When a contact finally answers, you will often learn that they are not a good contact for you.

- *Find the correct decision maker* – Aside from creating an opportunity or setting an appointment, this may be the best outcome for a call. You are likely calling into organizations that employ thousands of people across vast geographies. Those employees and departments are likely very siloed. Identifying the best decision maker to discuss your solution with is a huge win.

- *Find the incumbent(s)* – Aside from learning the best decision maker, this may be the most valuable piece of information. Understanding who you're up against will help guide your prospecting and opportunity strategies. (Of course, this assumes you know your competition very well—which you do—right?) In a previous role, I had a competitor and knew exactly their greatest weaknesses. I loved finding accounts which that competitor held and exploiting those weaknesses. I also knew my strong competitors and if they had enough tenure at a prospect account, I was often forced to deprioritize the prospect.

- *Get practice* – Prospecting is a skill that you can master through practice and repetition. You may be familiar with the 10,000-hour rule, which states that it takes 10,000 hours of practice to become expert at a skill. Malcolm Gladwell states that he considers this the key to success in any field.[11] The more you prospect the more you will improve finer aspects of what you say, when you call, how often you call, whom you call, and so forth. Making calls is in itself is a win because you are sharpening your prospecting skills.

- *Develop your messaging* – Along this line, your messaging will become crisper and more automatic and you can get better at tailoring your messaging to the people you call on. I once had a sales leader who was known for his ability to state a lengthy value proposition in a very natural and fast manner. At the time I thought I could never deliver our message as he did, but with practice, over a fairly short period, I was able to develop this skill myself. This should be your experience as well.

- In *Born to Win,* Zig Ziglar reflects on how often he practices his messaging.[12] Although his speech was memorized, he would still practice for several hours before every event and could deliver parts of his message and change the duration of the message on command.

- *Plant seeds* – I hear different numbers thrown out around how many calls it takes to reach a prospect. The article "21 Mind-Blowing Sales Stats" states the average is eight.[13] I have not taken the time to examine this research and it will be different for sales and business development people working in different capacities, but I think we can all agree that it usually takes multiple attempts to connect with your prospect.

One reason for this is that people usually need to see your name and company multiple times before engaging with you. Marketo's website states that "Lead nurturing is the process of developing relationships with buyers at every stage of the sales funnel, and through every step of the buyer's journey."[14] In the prospecting phase you are likely near the beginning of the buyer's journey, since you will create the opportunity when you contact the prospect. Now is the time when they are seeing your company's name in messaging, perhaps for the first time, and they need to be walked through the process many refer to as "lead nurturing." Your prospecting calls are part of this campaign. When you are prospecting, you are planting seeds in the prospect's mind that your company is a viable partner.

After starting in my first enterprise role, I remember calling my manager after a two-week drought of appointment setting and expressing to him my concern about my lack of success. He immediately responded that enterprise sales is like that—you may go longer periods of time without creating a new opportunity or setting a meeting. It can be tough to keep your attitude positive and your motivation level high during these droughts, so be kind to yourself and acknowledge the fact that you are doing many things that are contributing to your success. You may win opportunities years down the road and realize that the calls you make today are what started creating that opportunity.

ONE SHOT

I will never forget the time that I got through to a member of senior management at one of my key prospects. I was making calls in a careless manner and did not expect him to pick up the phone. When he did, I stumbled, and my messaging came out very poorly. I also did not have a specific reason to call him. He just said that he wasn't interested, and I could not argue. That was my one shot with him. I failed. Maybe I could call him a year or two after that hoping he wouldn't remember my name or my company, but I had fumbled the one chance I got with him. A peer of mine made the exact same mistake. A central decision maker of a Fortune 100 company answered the phone when he was in a mindless dialing mode and he was surprised when the prospect answered. He stumbled in his messaging. You may only get one shot with your named prospects and since you don't have many of them, each shot matters that much more.

The more you know about your prospects the better. This is where we leverage the work you did in Chapter Two. If I would have been on my prospecting A game when my prospect picked up the phone, I would have opened by citing something about a new product release from my prospect, something relevant in the industry, some way that he and I were connected—something that gets his attention, shows I called for a very specific reason, and that I know why I'm calling and how it benefits him. My colleague should have been able to do the same. Our one shot with our key prospects would have had a much higher chance of producing something valuable if we had been prepared and paying attention.

SLOW PLAY

When your prospects do not respond to your calls and emails, how often should you follow up? This likely depends on the personality of the prospect, timelines involved with your solution, the fiscal time of year, and many other factors, but something I want to emphasize is that you should not pester your prospects. The longer you stay in an industry the smaller it gets. You start to see the same people repeatedly and whether you know it or not you are building a relationship with those people.

This is usually not the case in SMB sales. In SMB sales you have way more prospects and it often makes sense to pressure the opportunity or prospect to a point where they move forward, or they are pushed out of your prospecting list. In enterprise sales, you have a limited number of prospects and opportunities. You should slow play those relationships because if your solution doesn't make sense for a prospect now, it certainly may in one, two, or several years from now. Always be gracious and polite because you may work with that contact in the future—even if they are at a different company down the road.

People are building unconscious ideas of you and those ideas will dictate how they respond to you. Your prospects form an opinion about you and your company from your calling frequency, urgency, and tone. Much of their response will be unconscious but it will still inform their reactions to you. In *Nudge,* Richard Thaler and Cass Sunstein talk about the Automatic and the Reflective systems of thinking—referred to as system one and system two in psychology literature, respectively.[15]

FISHING FOR WHALES

People's automatic system (system one) is informed by tone of voice, word choice, and body language, and people make the majority of their decisions using system one. When your calls become too frequent and your messaging too urgent and threatening, your contact's system one is likely to react defensively.

I once pestered a key prospect to the point that I was embarrassed to see her when we met again years down the road. The opportunity to partner with her organization came to me quickly. After discussing the potential partnership with a colleague, I scheduled a red eye flight that same day and was meeting with this prospect within a few days. The meeting went well to the extent that we had clear next steps on how my solution was going to fill a need they had. We completed one of the items in our next steps after the meeting. After that the prospect went completely silent. I couldn't believe it. It seemed like we had decent rapport and it seemed like a solid opportunity. I probably called her twenty times within the next six months. I even left candid messages asking for some type of clarification on the opportunity. She never called back.

About two years later I learned why when I crossed paths with her. She had engaged with a competitor of mine that she had known personally for many years. The timing was perfect for that competitor and she trusted my competitor more than me because of the tenure of their relationship. Sure, she should have extended enough curtesy to let me know she killed our opportunity, but I can't control her actions. I could control the number of times I reached out and my tone when doing so. Due to other circumstances, that prospect started working with a colleague of mine and I just knew that I had not left a good impression after making all those calls. I regretted making too many calls and using a stern tone. I have not made the same mistake since.

Of course, all opportunities are different, and the amount of follow-up calls required will vary greatly, but with cold calling you might think about making no more than one set of calls per quarter or even once per half. Call them, follow with an email and often a LinkedIn message. A couple days later follow again with a call and an email, then you might follow with one last e-mail. Then leave them alone for about three to six months. There is a balance here between making enough noise to be heard but not yelling so loudly that people permanently put you on mute.

When we are new to sales, we are often taught that prospecting activity leads to opportunities and opportunities leads to wins. Hence, sales management via activity metrics is a common practice. This is rightfully so in SMB sales. With a straightforward solution that is more of a commodity or a one-size-fits-all, sales management by activity metrics works. This approach does not work in large account sales and if you try and build your pipeline only through increased activity, you are not only spinning your wheels—you may be going backwards. Do your research. Take every call seriously. Celebrate the little wins and remember that your career in large account sales is a marathon and not a sprint.

CHAPTER SIX:
BE A CONSULTANT

n this chapter, we will explore custom messaging as the foundation for setting meetings. We will review examples of custom solutions and messaging.

The principle in this chapter is:

- Customize Every Call

You are providing a complex solution and you should approach the prospect as a consultant. Everyone tells salespeople to be a consultant—consultant is the big buzz word. I see organizations that title their sales rolls as consulting rolls. But what does consulting consist of? Even if your solution does not have a lot of complexity, it will likely be a complex undertaking for an enterprise prospect to incorporate your solution into their existing way of doing things. Your prospects need to help with your company's specific solution and also with how to best leverage your type of solution. So, you must give them expert advice. Yes, you will actively listen to your prospects from first contact and throughout the sale, but you will approach them as an industry expert who is bringing an idea, a concept—a new way of doing things. This is what consulting is in large account sales. A consultant must be the new you.

A great example of large account consulting is in *Trailblazer* by Mark Benioff. Benioff tells his story of how he approached Toyota with a complex solution that his company could deliver.[16] You could say Toyota was on Benioff's prospect list because Benioff states that he always admired the company. When he saw Toyota struggling with public opinion due to the stuck accelerator fiasco, he developed a solution custom for Toyota's unique needs at the time and asked for a meeting to present this solution. He got that meeting and presented his custom solution. He was consulting with Toyota and using his company's products as the central solution.

As a consultant, you will get prospects to meet with you by helping them see their problems and solutions more clearly. Information is abundant. Giving prospects facts does not add enough value for you to get a meeting. You must help your prospect see that they have a problem. Daniel Pink calls this "clarity."[17] "The ability to move others hinges less on problem solving than problem finding."[18] You need to be a problem solver, but in the appointment setting stage, just finding problems can get you the meeting.

Combine the consultant role with someone who is able and willing to tell prospects what their problems are and provide a solution, and you have a personal profile that fits Matthew Dixon and Brent Adamson's "The Challenger." In *The Challenger Sale*, we are introduced to a new profile of sales rep, called "The Challenger."[19] Dixon and Adamson arrive at five profiles of sales reps and, although you may be of a different profile, you may be able to leverage some of the tools of The Challenger. The Challenger:

- Always has a different view of the world

- Understands the customer's business
- Loves to debate
- Pushes the customer[20]

In order to bring new value to your prospect, look at her business differently. Be willing to argue against her current solutions and push her to do better. Note that these skills are particularly helpful in a down economy.[21] As you adopt this consultative approach, your messaging will stand out because it will be customized. This is Principle 11.

PRINCIPLE 11: CUSTOMIZE EVERY CALL

Leverage the work you do in Chapters Two and Three and develop a unique message for each prospect. "Read this slowly: prospective customers are not interested in what you do. They are interested in what you do for them . . . Stop talking about your yourself and your company and begin leading with the issues, pains, problems, opportunities and results that are important to your prospect,"[22] says Mike Weinberg. I love the straightforward language Weinberg uses here toconvey the essential truth about enterprise prospecting—put forth here as Principle 11. Lead with something unique to your prospect and that will help your prospect.

You will see something in the marketplace or in your research that triggers an idea, which allows you to bring value in a way that only you can, and you will call the customer asking to present this idea. Your ideas should be new, fresh, and innovative. Here are some common places in which to root your thinking:

- *A different way of thinking about your solution* – Products go to market with a core concept and then often branch out from that core concept. Under Armour clothing started as a specialty product worn under athletic gear and in no time was manufacturing everything from shoes to hats as well. Vari, formerly known as Varidesk, started as a desktop solution and soon was manufacturing other office components like walls, seating, and entire desks.

Your company's solution may already have these branches and these branches are a great way to start a conversation with your prospects. They may not know about these additional capabilities and these capabilities may be just what your customer needs. If your company has not created these additional solutions, check with management and see when they are coming.

- *Reconfigure or use your solution in a different way* – Companies find ways to pivot, when forced to, in order to maintain growth. They change, enhance, create partnerships, merge, acquire, and create new solutions. Copy machines sellers began providing IT solutions alongside the copy machine, as the demand for copy machine solutions decreased. This pivot was organic because the copy machine sat on the IT network and copy machine sellers were already in touch with the IT contacts at their customer accounts. Accounting firms also began providing IT solutions in order to grow revenue.

  How does your solution deliver value, apart from the most common ways? In our ERP example in Chapter One, John finds that human resources departments can reduce spending with some unique features of his solution. He shows how to use his solution in a different way.

- *Fill a need that is new to the world or industry* – During the COVID-19 pandemic, manufacturers of other security devices began creating fever detection systems. Healthcare imaging manufacturers began creating machines to detect diseases.

  Look for unfolding needs in the marketplace and find ways that your solution can meet those needs. A word of caution here—beware fleeting trends. News purveyors love making stories that end up fizzling quickly. Don't chase short-lived needs. You may get some interest from talking about these needs, but, for a company to invest, the solution need needs to have some long-term use.

- *Reduce spend* – Reduction in overhead is great for the bottom line. Technology solutions often reduce the fat, as do other forms of management consulting. If your solution can reduce your prospect's spend—potentially even beyond the cost of your solution—well then, it's a no-brainer, right?

- *Increase Revenue* – I once called on a prospect and I claimed that my solution can help increase their sales. The prospect replied that they were not looking to increase their sales! I don't think they were putting me off or being sarcastic. Their explanation was that they were working on their infrastructure just to support the business they already had and could not take on new business.

  I believe this was the only time I've ever had a prospect tell me they were not interested in increasing revenue. While not always priority one, increasing revenue is almost always attractive to organizations. How does your solution increase revenue?

- *Reduce the amount of time it takes to review data* – Business intelligence solutions have become a major industry. Your product likely has some type of business intelligence feature built in. This feature may be important to some of your prospects.

- *Increase available capital* – Finance companies are eager to lend money. Available capital, or cash on hand, can help a company's bond rating and a company's stock price. Capital can be used to generate new revenue and improve a company's bottom line in many ways.

- *Increase workflow efficiency* – How many meetings have you been on with multiple people, to which someone is late? How much does it cost your company for each person attending a meeting to wait five minutes to start because someone is late? When I consider the need to schedule a meeting, I think seriously about the cost to my company, in using people's time, for those meetings. Workflow efficiency is a massive factor that does not get enough attention.

   How much money is your time and your colleague's time worth? Invaluable, yes—but I mean to your employer's bottom line. According to your income and your goals, what is your time worth per hour? What is your manager's time worth and what is your CEO's time worth?

   If your solution can increase efficiency for your prospects, there is a lot of value there and this is a great place to adopt a challenger approach and help your prospects see how increasing efficiency can impact their bottom line.

- *Reduce the spend of a given solution* – "Why would someone purchase our solution?" The room was quiet. A sales leader had posed the question to a room I was in. One brave soul spoke up and said, "to save money!" What she said is what everybody was thinking, and everybody was wrong. Our solution was not cheaper than the competition, but young salespeople often think that the biggest, or only, reason to change solutions is to save money. Perhaps this is because the value in reducing spending is so obvious. Reducing spend is fantastic and if a company can save enough money and the risk and resources to do so are reasonable, they often will move forward.

   I once talked with a CFO evaluating a purchase—well into six figures in cost. His team presented three solutions from the largest manufacturers in the business—all with great reputations in delivering quality products. He told me that to him they were all the same. He felt each proposal would fulfil his company's need and he was only concerned with the spend. While not fun for salespeople, the cost of the solution is a consideration for the buyer.

You need a unique reason to call your prospects. Your customers can evaluate products all day long on their own. They don't need you to call them just to tell them facts about your products. They need you to give them ideas, advise them on best practices with your solution, and challenge them to find more effective ways of doing business. They need you to be a consultant and will accept you as one. When you act as a consultant, your messaging will be customized and in turn your calls will carry a unique message that sets you apart. Another way of customizing your call is citing your prospect's or industry news.

By citing news about your prospect or their industry, you will stand out from all the noise in their inbox. How many solicitation emails do you get per day that read something like "Our product just won the gold award!" or "We can give you ABC," or "Here is some information on XYZ," and so on and so on. These forms of messaging are more of an information push. Even if I happen to be in the market for exactly one of these products, I am unlikely to read this e-mail because my sourcing of the product will be deliberate and organized and I would not be dissuaded to read a one-off email.

In contrast, put yourself in your prospect's shoes. Think like your prospect. What if you are your prospect and you just released a new product that is all the buzz internally. At the same time, you receive a message that reads "Congratulations on the release of your [specific name of product]" or "Sales strategy for your [specific name of new product]" or "Increase your profitability on your [specific name of product]." If that message names your new product by name in the subject line, it will at least get your attention. It will likely get you reading the message—if only the first two to three lines. What if your industry experienced a substantial change such as new laws, market movement or acquisitions—something substantial that is on your mind. You receive a timely email stating "[Specific] Industry headline matters, let's discuss." I believe you will click on those emails and at least take a glance at the message. If that message resonates with you, you might respond, and even take the meeting.

Name dropping is another way to get your prospect's attention. You are at a trade show, a prospect event, or some other industry event, and you meet somebody who suggests you talk to someone specific in their company. Get that referring person's name and let them know you'll mention them by name. Then call and email your contact, mentioning the referring person by name.

If your company has a history with your prospect, mention that in your call and email and that may get your prospect's attention. You may have noticed that many solution providers out there claim they provide their services to a high percentage of the Fortune 500 or the Fortune 1000. How is it possible that so many solution providers service most of the Fortune 500? Often, they provided these customers one free widget, or they sold several widgets to a single branch. This gives them the ability to claim they work with that company. Your company may have some type of transactional history with your prospects. Investigate this and when you find this to be the case, lead with this when soliciting your prospects.

John Medina's Brain Rule #4 is that "We don't pay attention to boring things."[23] Your prospects are interested in themselves, including their goals, challenges, and initiatives. Stand out in their cluttered inbox by talking to them about themselves, their company, products, industry, peers, and other things that are personal, or at least close, to themselves. Do this to get their attention. Get their attention in order to approach them with a critical solution. You have been watching them and believe you have a solution to help. When you do get the meeting, there will be a balance between presenting the solution that you lead with and listening to your prospect's needs. Pivot appropriately.

CHAPTER SEVEN: FORMS OF PROSPECTING

In this chapter, we will discuss how and when to prospect via the telephone, written messaging and in-person.

The three principles in this chapter are:

- Use your telephone to cold call
- Use written messaging to compliment telephone calls
- Prospect in person

Your modes of prospecting on large account sales are a combination of phone calls, written messaging, and in-person prospecting. Yes, I advocate calling prospects with your telephone, as do many top sales consultants, most successful large account sales executives, and most enterprise sales management. Calling prospects and leaving voicemails is a fantastic way to get their attention. Often, they respond to your emails and LinkedIn messages, but many times they were directed to your email because you called them. It was the voicemail that prompted their notice of your written message. The phone call is a powerful prospecting tool in large account sales, and you should use it. Messaging and prospecting at events are your other modes of prospecting to large accounts.

USE YOUR PHONE

Cold calling via telephone calls has become rare. This is all the more reason to use your telephone to cold call. There are a lot of arguments against cold calling and many people screaming "Cold calling is dead." I will admit that some organizations—especially some of the big tech companies—have made it pretty much impossible to cold call into their organization because contacting their employees via telephone does not seem to be possible at all. Furthermore, as a result of COVID-19, I am seeing more robust, self-serve websites and portals, and fewer telephone connections to company employees. This rise in customer service being delivered via technology rather than by people makes cold calling more challenging.

Perry Marshall stated that "Cold calling is dead"[24] in his book *80/20 Sales and Marketing* published several years ago! If cold calling was dead then, it must be mummified by now. In his book *80/20 Sales and Marketing*, Marshall has a lot of good ideas about how to generate warm leads and he asserts that one should only call on warm leads.[25] I like warm leads, too, and I don't think anyone would argue that an organization needs to have marketing media, advertising, and various forms of mass communication that help generate warm leads. There are lots of creative ways of generating warm leads. I liked the article "3 Proven Ways To Get In Front of Decision Makers," by Ago Cluytens, in which he shows how to use research to generate meetings.[26] In this article, he argues that cold calling can work but it doesn't work enough of the time. I agree that you will need to find some channel for inbound leads and in my experience, from my very first sales job out of school to today, about half of my opportunities come from cold calling and half come from inbound channels. All this said, cold calling is not dead and never has been, and likely never will be.

PRINCIPLE 12: USE YOUR PHONE TO COLD CALL

Success in sales without cold calling is, as Jeb Blount puts it, "Fantasy Island."[27] Judging from my experience and what I've seen my peers do over the years, about half of your opportunities will come from picking up the phone and calling somebody who you do not know, in order to start a conversation. Konrath states that "The phone needs to be your primary tool to get your foot in the door of big companies."[28] Time and technology have of course affected the way we interact. Yet, advancements have not wholesale changed the way enterprise sales and BD execs find new opportunities. Konrath published that statement even before Marshall—about fourteen years ago—but Blount's statement was published a year after Marshall's. Now, in this culture and economy, is a great time to cold call.

There is a table in *Selling to the C-Suite* which has five different modes of connecting with senior management and corresponding percentages of success.[29] Cold calling by telephone alone has a fair degree of success in this table and when combined with written communication the percentage of success goes up. (We will cover cold calling in combination with written communication in the next principle.) Furthermore, how do you connect with people in order to get referrals? I'm sure you have an existing network but in order to grow that network you will likely need to, again, pick up the phone and use it to cold call. In Section Three, we will see multiple examples of large accounts sales wins that started with a cold phone call. Cold calling via telephone works and should be central to your prospecting. You should combine written communication with the phone call.

PRINCIPLE 13: USE WRITTEN MESSAGING
TO COMPLIMENT TELEPHONE CALLS

Follow your call and voicemail with some type of written communication, like email, LinkedIn message, text, snail mail, or messaging in other media. Konrath,[30] and Read and Bistritz[31] advise supporting your telephone campaign with written communication. Starting a written conversation makes it easier for your contact to respond. The combination of voice and written communication is more likely to get your prospect's attention. Writing custom messages every time is a must. Use formats other than email, like LinkedIn messaging, messaging via other media, texting, and snail mail. This will certainly set you apart from other solicitors.

When you follow your telephone message or voicemail with an email, text, or LinkedIn message, it makes it easier for your prospect to respond to you. Picking up the phone and calling someone back is a big ask. If you have piqued your prospect's interest, their next move with you is likely to hear more of what you have to say. If they can simply accept a meeting request with a time that works for them, they are more likely to engage you. They may have a simple question which they can ask by responding to your email. They may let you know why they are not a good fit in a response and do you the favor of disqualifying themselves as a prospect. Sometimes they will respond with a nugget of intel that will go a long way, like who the incumbent is or the correct contact for you in their organization. Give your prospect the easy response format of written communication, after you get their attention with phone calls and voice messages.

Go fishing for whales. How many spam emails do you get daily? Your prospects get a ton. Their senior management titles increase the amount of spam in their inbox. They are likely to recognize your email as spam and delete or block your address permanently. If you start with a voice message, they are more likely to read your written message.

This is like a fly-fishing technique in which you use an attractor fly, followed by a fly that imitates what the fish actually eats. Sometimes the fish will bite the attractor fly, but the real value in that first, large, loud attractor fly is that it gets the fish's attention. Once you have the fish's attention, it is more likely to take the real bait. Your phone call is the attracter fly. Get your prospect's attention with the less common, louder voice message so that they respond to the written message and take a meeting with you.

Every voice and written message should be custom, *every single time.* I know, this is not efficient. You probably used scripts and templates in SMB prospecting. In enterprise sales, you must cite timebound intel specific to your prospect's company, products, or industry, with every communication. How many emails per day do you get from companies stating what they are so good at and the awards their products have received? Don't be one of those companies. Sure, your prospects will need to learn how your company is capable at delivering excellent solutions, but that comes later. When you are first asking for a conversation, cite something happening with your prospect that your solution will help with. This is where you execute and leverage that ongoing research you are doing and why we have Principle 5: know your prospects inside and out.

Before ever making a call, have a plan for what your specific message is going to be for this prospect. Then, pick up the phone and dial. You will very likely get the contact's voicemail, or, potentially, a personal assistant. Your message should be confident, very brief, and state why you are calling—to present to them how you can increase ABC, decrease XYZ, etc. *Tell them you are sending an email* and look forward to discussing. Then, immediately send your email while the plan is fresh in your mind.

In your message's subject line, reference the product, company or industry news that have informed your solution. This will get their attention. In the body of the email, reference the voicemail you left. Write briefly how your solution may be able to support their efforts, with respect to the product, company or industry news in your subject line. Then ask for a meeting. If you did indeed get their attention and the timing is right, you will either get the meeting or be referred to the person with whom you should meet. By the way, don't include attachments or links. These are both flags for fishing emails and other cybersecurity concerns and your email will be stopped by their firewall.

Texting is a written medium you might use, and I agree with Jeb Blount that you should use it only with someone whom you have met or who have some familiarity with you.[32] Don't text someone you do not know. Do use texting whenever you can with active prospects who you have met. I have had prospects text me before I had texted them and I was surprised that they wanted to take our engagement to that more private, less formal platform. If emails compliment phone calls, texting compliments in-person and after-hours engagements. If you met with someone in a less formal place, like a trade show or for lunch, move your dialogue to texting. If they asked you to contact them outside of standard business hours or when you know they are out of the office, text them. I love it when I can text with a prospect because we all get fewer business messages in our text inbox than in our email inbox. I know that when I text them, they see it right away. When you do get to this stage with a prospect, don't abuse it.

The last form of the written word I want to discuss is LinkedIn messages. As an enterprise sales or BD executive, you should be leveraging LinkedIn's paid-for services for research, as well as communication. Messages to first-degree connections are free. With some premium LinkedIn subscriptions, you get a set number of monthly messages which you can send to prospects, with whom you are not connected. These messages are very similar to an email format and provide plenty of characters for any prospecting message you would want to send. Your contacts receive fewer LinkedIn messages than emails, so your message stands out. It's a different platform, and so may be more likely to gain your prospect's attention. Some say that people are more likely to read LinkedIn messages than email. While people advocating the use of LinkedIn messages are probably interested parties,[33] you might consider some of the advantages to using LinkedIn mail alongside email.

The combination of a phone call plus the written message is the key to starting dialogue, in part because it gets your prospect's attention and makes it convenient for them to respond to you. Make your message completely custom every time and when texting, only do so when you have had some contact with the prospect. One form of written communication that I did not bring up is snail mail. I have seen sales executives mail thank you cards, letters, choochkies, and quirky gifts to get people's attention. Konrath[34] and Read and Bistritz[35] mentioned this as an effective method of prospecting. Again, the key to leveraging this form of written communication is to combine it with the telephone call. There may be opportunities using communication on other social media platforms, like Slack, Facebook, Twitter, Instagram, or others. There is likely opportunity for large account prospecting in those mediums for you as well.

PROSPECT IN PERSON

Prospecting in person requires a substantial investment in your time and the dividends may not pay for years. Nonetheless, you will get so much value from prospecting in person that I recommend you do it. You may end up running a successful meeting with your prospects when prospecting in person. More likely you will gain valuable information and meet people who can help you—both employees of your prospect account and industry influencers.

When prospecting in person, use Evernote or OneNote on your phone, in order to take notes. This allows you to jot down important bits of information before your forget, in an efficient and nondescript manner. Rather than taking out a pen and writing on the back of someone's business card, or pulling a notepad out of our backpack and setting up office, you can simply step aside and get important information down before you forget it. Best practice here is to create a table in Evernote or OneNote, in which your prospect has a section. An example of a prospecting table for trade shows is the in appendix.

I am writing this during the "safer-at-home-phase" of COVID-19 and the future of large gatherings is in question. Even so, I do have a list of trade shows to attend in the next year—both virtual and in-person. Apart from large gatherings, smaller gatherings and drop-ins to your prospect's offices may provide a platform for in-person prospecting.

PRINCIPLE 14: PROSPECT IN PERSON

Meet people in person in order to learn more about them and their level of interest in working with you, and in order to have higher value conversations than what you get over the phone. People communicate more through body language, eye contact, and facial expressions than through the words they speak. Through your prospect's physical language, you can learn so much more about what are saying, as well as what they are not willing to explicitly tell you. I recall a prospect that I never met with in person. Not meeting with him in person strained the relationship. His tone of voice on the phone suggested a lack of enthusiasm, but over time I saw that his actions suggested he was an enthusiast for my solution. This made the interaction confusing for me.

If I were to meet with him, perhaps his body language and facial expressions would tell me something. I could learn more about his personality and manner that could clarify this seemingly contradictory behavior. In contrast, I had a prospect that I met with many times via in-person meetings. Meeting with him in person really helped me understand his decisions. A couple of his decisions fell short of what I was hoping to achieve. I did not understand these decisions, from his logical argument alone. After meeting with him in person, I better understood his motivations. He communicated certain preferences and biases to me during our in-person meetings, via body language, eye contact, and facial expressions. One reason why I like prospecting at trade shows is so I can gauge the prospect's level of actual interest in my solution by observing their body language and eye contact. Furthermore, people will give you more time, commitments, and information in person than over the phone.

Prospecting at trade shows is costly and it is a big time commitment but the results are often substantial and worth the investment. Opportunities from prospecting at trade shows include the following:

- *Meet people who can introduce you to your ultimate sponsor* – Ultimate decision makers often times do not attend a trade shows. But lots of other people do and you can often meet someone in middle management at a trade show, who can in turn introduce you to the right people. That introduction is oftentimes the key to getting the meeting you need with your prospect. In *Selling to the C-Suite*, we learn that a recommendation from someone in their own company is the best way to gain access to the C-Suite.[36]

- *Big value in attending and not exhibiting* – Exhibiting at a trade show may be the right answer for you. However, the general consensus that I have gathered from people who exhibit is that exhibiting is more of a branding and marketing necessity that major industry suppliers are required to fulfill. That is, they do not measure success in direct ROI only from sales. Sure, exhibitors are gathering leads and talking with prospects, but these major solution providers seem to consider exhibiting more of a marketing and advertising cost.

Likely, your best bet is to attend as "exhibit-only," or just attend the show without exhibiting. Mike Weinberg does the same,[37] and I know many salespeople who regularly attend trade shows, without exhibiting, and smart companies that send people to trade shows just to "walk the show," or attend only the exhibit hall.

- *Everyone in one place* – If your prospects are aligned by industry, you likely have multiple prospects in one place at trade shows. Even if you are targeting only the largest companies in an industry, you may have five or more premier prospects in one place at the same time. That concentration of prospects represents huge opportunity. You can pursue that opportunity in a very efficient manner while they are all under the same roof.

- *Gain prospect knowledge* – I have learned more valuable information in a prospect's booth then I have in making years of phone calls or doing online research. People will be more open to you in a face-to-face engagement. When you approach someone in person, they are obliged to talk to you, at least for a moment. In that moment, you can find out who is the best contact, who is the incumbent, and what is the company's general attitude and approach around your solution.

- *Gain industry knowledge* – Sales and business development people often attend only the exhibit floor at a trade show. Alternatively, it may make sense for you to get a full trade show pass and attend sessions. Some shows only offer full passes and so you should take advantage of the opportunity to attend sessions, but you might even invest in purchasing a full pass in order to gain industry knowledge. You can view the agenda and pick out which sessions will help you learn aspects of your prospect's industry that are most applicable to your solution.

- *Advantage over competition* – If you are there, some of your competition is likely there. But most of your competition probably is not. This gives you an advantage. It shows your prospects that you and your company are committed enough to invest in your attendance at that show. If you did get face time with a prospect, that can go a long way and put you ahead of your competitors that are just calling your prospect.

- *Pre-show information* – Trade shows are generally very organized and offer a great deal of information prior to the show. This information includes what companies are exhibiting and where. Rather than just showing up and walking the aisles, do research prior to the show as to who your targets are and where they are. This will increase your efficiency at the show and therefore increase your ROI.

I have had several instances of walking into a large prospect's booth at a trade show, asking for a person who I can talk to about my solution, and getting a lengthy meeting right then and there with the final decision maker. This does happen at trade shows. Much more often, however, you will gather a lot of very valuable information that will help you in your prospecting after the show.

Trade shows are not the only place to prospect in person. Other platforms at which to prospect in person include the following:

- *Company events* – Large companies often have events in which their customers, some of their employees, vendors and partners attend. Oftentimes they help fund these events by allowing vendors to pay for a table or selling guest passes. Some of these events are more intimate than trade shows and you may get more access to decision makers at smaller, more intimate events.

- *Speaker events* – Authors and industry influencers hold speaking engagements that may attract a subset of people, which may include people with whom you want to speak. For instance, Chip Conley held such an event in 2019 that a couple of my prospects were attending. I thought about attending that event in the hope that I might introduce myself to those prospects. I ended up not attending due to conflicting priorities, but the opportunity was there and I believe can be with similar events. Watch for events in which industry influencers are speaking and consider attending if only to meet your prospects in person.

- *Charity events* – I have attended several charity events in which I was able to speak with prospects. There is a cost to this and hopefully you find value in supporting that charity. The tone at these events may not be one where you try and pull someone aside and strike up a business conversation. The extra value is that your prospect will respect the fact that you are supporting the same charity that they are, and it will give you the opportunity to follow up with them later. Of course, you should attend charitable events that you sincerely want to support. Attending a charity that you conflict with could manifest friction between you and your prospects.

- *Industry socials* – Some trade organizations host events that are essentially a party. You pay to attend and tickets may be limited. Attend these events to increase rapport with existing prospects and gain more contacts at your prospect accounts. These are formats where people are having fun, are laid back and therefore more approachable, and you may learn a lot about how your solution is handled in your prospect's company. You will likely find some opportunity to talk business briefly. These are fun events and people are mostly getting to know each other, so keep shop talk to a minimum.

- *Drop offs* – A drop off is when you physically walk into a prospect's location and give them a physical object. The object may be food, a folder with your company's info, or something creative meant to leave an impression. You ask to give it to your contact in person, but if you cannot do that, you leave it for that person and follow up via phone and email. This is a seldom practiced prospecting technique in enterprise prospecting, and yet, I have seen it work.

A good example of this comes from a friend of mine in the software space. On a personal vacation, he dropped into a prospect's headquarters, where the president of the company has his office, carrying a box full of warm muffins. He walked into the office, approached the receptionist and asked for his contact, to hand him the muffins. The receptionists asked the contact if he would like to receive the muffins, and the president agreed and came to the lobby. My friend introduced himself, stated the company he worked for, and that he knew the incumbent. He stated he would appreciate the opportunity to educate the president on what he thinks he can do for the prospect's company. The prospect stated that he was impressed with his fortitude and committed to giving him an hour. Starting with that hour, he won that business. He, of course, handed over the muffins first.

Modes of prospecting in large accounts are mostly the same as in SMB sales. Perhaps the telephone is used more in SMB prospecting. Networking for leads is more effective in SMB and less effective with large accounts. Certainly, call metrics look very different in large account sales. But in any case, the modes of prospecting in large account sales are essentially the same as in SMB sales.

Depending on your personality and what you enjoy, you will likely use some modes more than others. I am fairly successful on the telephone. I have seen some use networking to great effect, and I have seen others bring in incredible wins by dropping into their prospect's offices! I am sure that you will use a combination of all these modes. Some enterprise sales executives have been in their industry for a long time. They have such an extensive network that their cold calling days may be over. For those people, attending industry events and keeping up with existing contacts may be all they need to keep a full prospect funnel. For the rest of us, we need to leverage all helpful tools. If you are new to an industry and your opportunity funnel is empty or low, the telephone is likely your best friend.

This concludes Section Two, in which we covered time management, how and how much to prospect, and some techniques and modes of prospecting to large accounts. Since you are already successful, you likely have some tools in place for managing yourself for success. Many salespeople are energetic and outgoing and lose track of time and details. However, as a true professional, as an executive, you need to manage yourself for maximum effectiveness. This includes managing when and how much you prospect and when and how much you research. Remember that large account sales is a long game and not a sprint, so learn as much as you can about your industry. Make enough noise to be noticed but not to be permanently muted by important people in your industry.

Become a smart, sophisticated consultant and use basic prospecting techniques. Bring thoughtful ideas and insights to your prospects, and you will get meetings. Just meeting with you and hearing your ideas will be valuable to your prospect. Of course, you need a way to get your prospect's attention in order to secure a meeting. That first connection is achieved through phone calls, emails, LinkedIn messages, in-person prospecting, and networking. You might also send attention-getting items via snail mail and leverage other social media platforms. Prospecting is certainly different in large account sales, but the platforms for prospecting are essentially the same as what is used in SMB prospecting.

SECTION THREE: CASE STUDIES: PROSPECTING PRINCIPLES IN ACTION

I chose to include a section on case studies to answer the question "Do these principles actually work? In real world scenarios? My job and livelihood are at stake." Section three contains four case studies that are true stories, which have taken place since 2010, and they demonstrate success using all the principles in this book. I want you to know that these principles work, and this section demonstrates the effectiveness of these principles. These stories are not exceptions to some rule that none of us know about or understand. These stories represent how deals get done as a result of prospecting to enterprise accounts.

CHAPTER EIGHT: PROSPECTING PRINCIPLES IN ACTION

In this chapter, we will see the principles of prospecting to large accounts used to create real sales opportunities.

The principles in this chapter are:

- Know Specifically how Your Solution Helps Customers
- Your Prospect List Should be Diverse
- Prospects Should Share Themes
- Know Your Prospects in Depth
- Start at the Top
- Do Background Research when Selecting Contacts
- Find Multiple Contacts
- Prioritize Prospecting Above all Else
- Do Less Prospecting
- Customize Every Call

- Use Your Phone to Cold Call
- Use Written Messaging to Compliment Telephone Calls
- Prospect in Person

In this chapter there are four case studies about prospecting to large accounts. Seeing the principles of prospecting to large accounts play out in true stories is an opportunity for you to validate these concepts in the real world, see more examples of how these principles can work, and see how these principles resonate through the conclusion of the sale. I hope you will derive some confidence and enthusiasm reading about these actual wins, which came from cold prospecting into large accounts.

The stories come from my experiences and sales executives that I know. The stories are told in the third person. Names and some details are changed in order to protect the privacy of parties related.

CASE STUDY ONE: THE NATIONAL NETWORK WIN

Principles Demonstrated:

- Principle 1: Know Specifically how Your Solution Helps Customers
- Principle 2: Your Prospect List Should be Diverse
- Principle 3: Prospects Should Share Themes
- Principle 7: Do Background Research when Selecting Contacts
- Principle 8: Find Multiple Contacts
- Principle 9: Prioritize Prospecting Above all Else
- Principle 10: Do Less Prospecting
- Principle 11: Customize Every Call
- Principle 12: Use Your Phone to Cold Call
- Principle 14: Prospect in Person

The Story:

James was hired by a technology company to bring on new customers in a direct sales model. The product was created for enterprise customers and James' background was in SMB sales. Although James was thoroughly trained on the product and was armed with sales tools and product knowledge, he was not given leads or much direction about to whom or where to prospect.

James spent the first month in product training and getting to know his team. He was motivated to sell this new solution in which he had a lot of confidence. His team's sales strategy was simply to cold call customers that appeared to use the solution he was selling. He and his team practiced their pitch and talked through prospecting experiences. They reviewed and fine-tuned a very professional presentation deck. He had a lot of support. When he found an opportunity, he would run an online presentation with the customer, and he had the people resources needed to help close the opportunity from there.

James knew the value of hard work and was committed to making prospecting calls, but he was not immediately successful. Day after day, James went into his cubicle and made prospecting calls. The problem was he was not finding good opportunities. People he talked to were usually not in the market to purchase his solution and when he did find someone that was in the buying process for his solution, his proposal was just added to a stack of other proposals. Discouraged, James added networking as a way to originate opportunities. This worked to a degree. James did get a small win after leveraging a warm introduction to a company that needed his solution. Although this was a small win and James was after larger wins, it gave James some momentum and yielded more success than what his team was having.

James knew something needed to change with his prospecting approach. After spending some time with his SVP, James started to understand in greater detail how his solution specifically helps their customers (Principle 1). With this understanding, James decided that he could target an industry which he believed had more need for his company's unique capabilities (Principle 3). He compiled a list of prospects within this industry and again started making phone calls (Principle 12). Although he grew tired of prospecting, he knew that the way to get relief from the work of prospecting was to find opportunities that got him out of the office. He stayed disciplined and made the phone calls (Principle 9).

In not much time, James found a lead that turned out to be a good one. James was making intentional, targeted calls (Principle 10) to prospects in his industry (Principle 11) and, from a cold call, he was referred to a prospect. This prospect would become a national channel for James' solution. James researched his company's history with this contact and learned that some people at his company had worked with this contact in the past (Principle 7). He leveraged this referral to set a meeting. The meeting went well, and James now had a good opportunity.

The prospect was structured in such a way that James would have a new, separate opportunity at each of the prospect's locations. His contact, who was becoming his sponsor, was not the final decision maker for every location, but she could introduce James to the decision makers at every location. James' sponsor made some introductions and James began meeting with decision makers at locations across the country. James won a couple sales this way and began to meet more and more people within the organization (Principle 8). James also attended an industry event in which many of these prospects were attending (Principle 14). He was filling his pipeline with opportunities. These opportunities were coming from referrals, and James was seen by prospects as someone who knew their business and had experience in their industry. This opportunity was unique in that there was diversity in his developing prospect list, since some prospects were large, and some were smaller (Principle 2). James won a good number of these opportunities within this national network.

Discussion on the Story :

James entered a new job where leads, territories, and opportunity origination was not defined. Companies arm their salespeople with great presentation tools, technology, personnel resources, and great products to sell, but the opportunity origination process is often not defined in enterprise sales. Definitions around territories or industries are usually assigned with teams of more than a few salespeople, but lead generation is often left up to the sales executive. In large account sales, you are usually expected to know how to find deals on your own. Perhaps the complexity of large account prospecting makes is impossible to define and make opportunity origination programmatic. Companies solve this by hiring talented and experienced salespeople and leave the process up to them. You are likely to run into a situation like the one James had to work through. SMB sales is more of a machine where leads and the prospecting approach is well defined and measured—not so in large account sales.

Once James focused his prospecting into an industry that would benefit from his company's unique capabilities, he created a great opportunity by cold calling, with his telephone, in a thoughtful, smart manner. James' cold calling worked because his approach was actually warm. He was able to get the information he needed to create the opportunity—the decision maker's name—because he presented himself as someone who knew the industry and could add value. He was able to get a meeting with that person for this reason and because he took the time to uncover the history between his company and the decision maker's. Since James acted as a true professional, showing up to the office and prioritizing this prospecting time, he created the opportunity.

Submersion in the industry, in research, and in attending industry events, allowed James to create and grow the opportunity. Prospects will talk to you when they believe the conversation itself is valuable to them. Before they even consider adopting your solution, they need to feel their initial time with you is good use of their time. If they believe that you can help them learn something about the challenges that face them, speaking to you is time well spent. James created and grew the opportunity because of this. By meeting prospects in person, at industry events, James presented himself as an expert within his prospect's sphere of interest.

CASE STUDY TWO: AN IN-PERSON PROSPECTING WIN AND HOW IT WAS SAVED BY LEVERAGING MULTIPLE CONTACTS

Principles Demonstrated:

- Principle 1: Know Specifically how Your Solution Helps Customers
- Principle 3: Prospects Should Share Themes
- Principle 4: Know Your Prospects in Depth
- Principle 7: Do Background Research when Selecting Contacts
- Principle 8: Find Multiple Contacts
- Principle 14: Prospect in Person

The Story:

Michelle was attending an industry event for which she was prepared to approach several prospects (Principle 14). Michelle sold content management software to healthcare companies (Principle 3). She worked from a list of about fifty prospects and six of them were attending this event. Michelle's goals were to approach all six prospects, talk to people who may be involved in purchasing her solution, and learn more about how her solution can benefit her prospects.

Michelle was able to have two great conversations with one of her prospects. She started a conversation with a manager of operations, whom she asked for by name because she believed this contact had used a similar solution in her previous position (Principle 7). Michelle believed her solution could help the operations team. Michelle obtained the operations manager's contact information and promised to follow up after the event. The operations manager suggested Michelle also talk to someone in marketing, who was also at the event. Michelle was able to connect with this marketing manager (Principle 8), who was in the process of finding a content management solution. Michelle had some ideas on how her solution could work specifically for this company (Principles 1 and 5) and the marketing manager agreed there could be a fit. They exchanged contact information and agreed to discuss more after the event.

Michelle came away from the event having found an exciting new opportunity but, as is often the case in large account sales, it would take Michelle almost a year to win this prospect's business. The marketing manager Michelle met was tasked with onboarding new content management software. This person would be Michelle's main point of contact throughout the sale.

Not long after the industry event, Michelle delivered virtual and in-person presentations to the marketing team, and during her in-person visit, Michelle was able to again connect with the operations manager whom she'd met at the industry event. At some point, the sales process slowed, and Michelle had trouble getting timely responses from the marketing manager. These gaps in communication became concerning and long enough that Michelle decided to leverage the contact she had made on the operations team. Michelle was sensitive that the marketing manager owned this purchase, but she was able to leverage the operations manager's enthusiasm for her solution. This operations manager became an influencer to the purchase by providing her feedback to her company on how she believed she could leverage Michelle's solution.

Michelle would find out that her prospect was formalizing the purchase of content management software into a formal RFP. Although disappointed, Michelle was not surprised and felt she was well positioned with a custom solution and multiple sponsors. Michelle and her team would work with the marketing manager to answer questions and provide information. When communication gaps occurred, Michelle sent the marketing manager examples of how her solution had benefited similar healthcare companies and other relevant, industry-specific information. After a about a year, Michelle and her team were told they were awarded the contract.

Discussion on the Story:

Her company's solution was well equipped and deserved the win, but Michelle deserved credit for finding the opportunity, creating relationships that kept her in the sale, and positioning her solution in a custom, unique manner. Michelle's story demonstrates the need for product and prospect intel. Her story shows the effectiveness of prospecting in person and the importance of developing multiple contacts.

This opportunity would not have started without Michelle's industry and prospect knowledge. Michelle had a specific game plan for how she was going to approach the industry event. Because she had done her homework in prospect and contact research, she was able to have quality conversations right there at the event. She acted as a consultant in her first conversations. Approaching her prospect with that kind of preparation impressed them and made it easy to work with Michelle.

Her story demonstrates that opportunities come from prospecting in person. Michelle got to the marketing manager because she was having a productive conversation with the manager of operations. They had hit it off and so the manager of operations was open and willing to refer Michelle to the decision maker for Michelle's solution. While this could happen over the phone, it is much more likely to happen in person. Because Michelle met this decision maker at an industry event, Michelle and her company's commitment to the industry was implied. Further, Michelle essentially skipped over a lot of early sales process by meeting with the decision maker on the spot and setting a meeting to further pitch her custom solution. These in person, rather than virtual, meetings likely carried a lot of weight in the customer's decision to onboard Michelle's solution.

Having multiple contacts may have saved this large account sale. Michelle followed her prospect's direction of the sales process and worked with the marketing manager, but her operations manager contact also supported Michelle and her company during the buying process. Having this other contact gave Michelle the advantage needed to win the RFP.

CASE STUDY THREE: WARM COLD CALLING AND ANOTHER SALE SAVED BY LEVERAGING MULTIPLE CONTACTS

Principles Demonstrated:

- Principle 1: Know Specifically how Your Solution Helps Customers
- Principle 3: Prospects Should Share Themes
- Principle 5: Know Your Prospects in Depth
- Principle 6: Start at the Top
- Principle 7: Do Background Research when Selecting Contacts
- Principle 8: Find Multiple Contacts
- Principle 9: Prioritize Prospecting Above all Else
- Principle 10: Do Less Prospecting
- Principle 11: Customize Every Call
- Principle 12: Use Your Phone to Cold Call

- Principle 13: Use Written Messaging to Compliment Telephone Calls

The Story:

Sarah had spent almost ten years in technology sales and for the last several years she was selling to large accounts. Sarah originated at least half of her opportunities through cold calling. She was big on researching her prospects and she understood the value of research when selling a specialized product. Sarah wasn't exactly a seasoned enterprise sales representative, but she was getting there and practiced a lot of the principles of prospecting to large accounts.

Sarah placed value in knowing the specialized applications of her product and how they can help her prospects (Principle 1). She found that she was more successful getting meetings when pitching very specific applications of her product. When Sarah started in large account sales, she would introduce the general aspects of her solution and found that she could not compete with long-term incumbents. In order to compete, Sarah identified a unique transaction history where a very small subset of her company's customers had leveraged a specific aspect of her solution. She looked closely at how her product had helped customers by talking to people involved with those transactions. She developed a specialized use case. Sarah took this use case to market and found reception. Focusing on this specialized solution also narrowed Sarah's prospect list (Principle 3).

Sarah's specialized solution could only help a handful of prospects. Because Sarah had a short list of prospects, she spent plenty of time researching prospect accounts and their contacts. She knew the size, geography, value proposition, and many aspects of the operations of her prospects (Principle 5). Sarah researched contacts before adding to her prospecting list (Principle 7). For one of her top prospects, Sarah added the COO. She added this gentleman based on his long tenure with the company and because her solution was inherently valuable for an operations strategy. Sarah knew that this prospect should be experiencing challenges that her specific solution could fix, and she went straight to the top calling on the C-Suite (Principle 6).

Sarah practiced regular, disciplined prospecting blocks in which she would call her prospects, executing a telephone call, and follow it with written messaging (Principles 9, 10, 11, 12, and 13). This is how she gained a meeting with the COO. Sarah had a prospecting time blocked out regularly on her schedule. During one of these prospecting sessions, Sarah called this COO. He did not answer. Sarah left him a short but specific voicemail on why she wanted to meet with him. She followed this voicemail with a LinkedIn message that was short and concise and asked for the meeting at a specific time. That same day the COO responded accepting the meeting. Sarah would spend a productive hour with him detailing how her solution could help his organization. They left the meeting with the COO tasked to discuss Sarah's solution with other members of his management team.

In the next meeting, Sarah would meet another member of the management team, a VP of Operations, and began working closely with him. Sarah appreciated working with the VP, but as things progressed, she started to understand that the VP's vision for her solution was more limited than what she had pitched to the COO. This would greatly reduce the size of her sale. After a very limited launch under the VP's direction, Sarah's sale was minuscule. Sarah operated according to the VP's direction until she was able to leverage other contacts, who helped her expand her solution and in turn grow her sale with their company.

Sarah met more contacts when working within the VP's scope, and she worked with these contacts to expand the use of her solution in the prospect's company. Sarah knew that she had to be careful to stay within the boundaries given by her project manager. Yet, she needed to expand her business. She was able to do both because more parties wanted to leverage her solution and she met these contacts in an organic matter, as a result of working with people that the VP assigned to her. It worked out that Sarah's new contacts, who also wanted to leverage her solution, reported back to the VP, asking for his blessing to use Sarah's solution. He allowed the expansion of Sarah's solution, which grew Sarah's sale, and, in the end, Sarah counted a nice win with a large prospect.

Discussion on the Story:

This case study demonstrates the use of almost all the principles of prospecting to large accounts. The story demonstrates that doing upfront research, in order to approach the prospect in an intelligent, professional, organized manner pays off. It is an example that picking up your phone and calling someone in senior management can and does yield viable opportunities. We see again in this case study the importance of developing multiple contacts at the prospect account.

Sarah's opportunity would never have been created if Sarah had not done a great deal of upfront research and planning. Large account prospecting requires grit. We often don't want to invest time and energy into an effort in which the odds of finding an opportunity have, in many cases, a very low chance of success. Especially during periods when prospecting has not revealed many new opportunities, it can feel like all that research and planning is just for long shots. Some of us have easier sales than others. Some of us can identify with poor odds, but large account sales is always about doing a lot of work for an opportunity that may or may not manifest. It may be tempting to skip the steps of research and planning before approaching the prospect. Do not give into this temptation because you will be received as just another salesperson.

Senior management will respect and respond to salespeople they see as delivering value in that first contact. Your insights are often unique from what management hears from their in-house team and from what they find in their own research. Exclusive ideas can hold a great deal of value, and your unique experience in the industry and with your prospect's competitors also holds value for your contact's management team. All that upfront research is important so that you know your prospect's business and team members in general, but the real value from your research comes when you are able to formulate solutions for your prospect's challenges.

Sarah was able to get a meeting through cold calling with senior management when she asked to deliver this type of solution. Her first contact had likely thought about or heard of how solutions like Sarah's could help him. By meeting with Sarah, he was able to spend an hour of his time evaluating the concept from a perspective that he could not get elsewhere. There is a lot of value in that one hour for him, even if he did not move forward with her solution. After listing to Sarah's voicemail and reading her LinkedIn message, this senior manager gathered that Sarah had a unique perspective in an area in which he had interest. Hence, just the experience of hearing Sarah's idea was valuable and a good use of his time.

Of course, this one contact was not the only person involved in on-boarding Sarah's solution. I am not aware of any purchase or part-nership that requires a single decision maker in business-to-business sales. Outside of a sole proprietorship, or a company with one em-ployee, people make decisions together. Even small purchases usually require at least a quick approval, even in very small business settings. A complex sale in a large account will certainly require many decision influencers and decision makers. Some of these decision makers and influencers will be involved because they are likely to have concerns about your solution and even oppose your solution. You can expect to meet these types of headwinds.

Sarah grew her solution despite the limitations put onto her. She did this by finding additional sponsors. She was able to do this without damaging the relationship with her assigned project manager. If she would have damaged the relationship with the project manager, she could have lost the opportunity all together. So there was some risk in her decision to grow the opportunity with additional sponsors. You will undoubtedly have similar scenarios and need to judge the benefits and risks for each opportunity.

Sarah's win demonstrates almost all the principles of prospecting to large accounts. All of her upfront research and planning got her the key meeting. She was able to get the opportunity by cold calling senior management. Her story shows that major account sales have multiple decision makers and influencers who can disrupt your momentum, and Sarah demonstrates one way of dealing with this disruption.

CASE STUDY FOUR: A FORTUNE 100 WIN

Principles Demonstrated:

- Principle 1: Know Specifically how Your Solution Helps Customers
- Principle 2: Your prospect list should be diverse
- Principle 3: Prospects Should Share Themes
- Principle 5: Know Your Prospects in Depth
- Principle 7: Do Background Research when Selecting Contacts
- Principle 8: Find Multiple Contacts
- Principle 9: Prioritize Prospecting Above all Else
- Principle 10: Do Less Prospecting
- Principle 11: Customize Every Call

The Story:

Matt was a senior sales executive for a company that manufactured a disruptive office product. His company was doing well despite economic headwinds and was actually doing well *because of economic headwinds*. This was because the product Matt sold was not traditional and could be leveraged more fluently with the challenges that faced his industry. Matt understood this about his product (Principle 1) and he looked for companies that would benefit from the non-traditional approach in which his company accelerated.

Matt focused on the technology space because he felt that his product would be best received there (Principle 3), but Matt also spent time in channels that could bring sales if his technology play did not yield results (Principle 2). Matt found that companies were changing the way they leveraged his solution (Principle 5) and, because of his company's unique capabilities, Matt believed he had found a niche to pursue that would be best received by technology companies. Matt developed a short list of targets in that industry and began prospecting to them.

Matt used Google alerts and LinkedIn messaging as his primary prospecting tools. He set up Google alerts that would tip him off when his prospects made a change that could trigger the unique use of his solution. Matt did use his phone to cold call, but some of his technology prospects did not have traditional phone trees and extensions. So, Matt leveraged LinkedIn messaging as his platform for prospecting (Principle 9) to those contacts (Principle 10). He also used LinkedIn to research contacts. Due to the size of his largest prospect, Matt found seven potential contacts (Principles 7 and 8) whom he felt could be decision makers for the purchase of his product, and who he thought could champion the concept of his solution.

From his LinkedIn messages, one of these contacts replied to Matt with the name of a person that manages Matt's solution. Matt then messaged this correct product manager, mentioning the name of the person who referred Matt. By mentioning the referring person's name in the subject line, Matt got the attention of the correct product manager and set a meeting with her.

Matt's meeting with the product manager went well, and Matt would continue to leverage two of the other contacts he found. His instinct that this prospect would leverage his disruptive solution turned out to be correct (Principle 11). His product manager contact confirmed the unique need that Matt had pinpointed and started purchasing Matt's product, in a limited capacity, to fill that need. To grow the sale, Matt continued to work with two other contacts that he'd made in his research on LinkedIn. Matt continued to grow the sale and counted a great win to a top prospect.

Discussion on the Story :

The first thing Matt did right was to know specifically how his solution could help customers. He recognized a unique capability in his solution that filled a particular need in the market. Because of this, he approached his prospects with insight, rather than a sales pitch, or the basic offering of a common product. We can assume that he received responses from his prospecting because his contacts perceived potential value in his messaging. Fortune 100 companies purchase all kinds of solutions, and they receive constant solicitations. Matt set himself apart because he had the right solution for them, at the right time, and he approached them with messaging that revealed this insight.

Next, Matt took the time to identify an industry, ideal prospects in that industry, and the right contacts at those prospect accounts. Once Matt identified a niche his company could fill, he did his research on where to take his insights. Finding the right companies, at the right time, gave him the highest odds of receiving interest from his solicitation and it maximized his time spent in prospecting. He knew relevant changes that were happening at his prospects because he was alerted via Google alerts. So he called with a timely, smart solution. Of course, Matt didn't just call the main number and ask to be transferred to the person who might handle the purchasing of his solution. He researched contacts in LinkedIn and once he was given a name, he used the name of the referring person to get the project manager's attention. He gathered these names in his CRM, kept his contacts updated on other sales in the company, and was able to grow his sales through multiple contacts.

Win stories like this one, from cold prospecting into large accounts, are everywhere because this is very often how business happens. I do find it a little surprising at times that business conversations between large companies can start this way—but why not? Yes, business often happens as a result of old relationships and warm introductions, but it also happens as a result of smart, professional, and organized so-licitation. Perhaps cold calling and unsolicited insight sharing have gotten a poor name because cold calling often does waste people's time. Cold calling is frequently the practice of making a large volume of blind calls, knowing that at some point you will get lucky and talk to someone. When a professional sales executive develops helpful insights and researches the appropriate parties to share this with, it's not the same as random cold calling—even when said sales executive has not met with or been invited to call on her prospect.

Yet again, we see the fruits that come from developing multiple contacts at prospect accounts. Matt started with a list of seven contacts. He started messaging and scheduled his first meeting by getting the name of an additional contact from someone on his original list. Due to the nature of his solution and the size of his prospect, he felt com-fortable reaching out to multiple contacts at his prospect. This helped grow his sale and, because he was able to share with his contact the progress that he was making with other contacts, his contacts developed an increased level of trust and security in working with him.

Matt won the business of a Fortune 100 company by identifying a unique need in the market and the fact that only his company could fill that need. His research and organization lead to the first meeting, and that first meeting was the result of cold calling via messaging.

Does reading Matt's story give you the confidence and enthusiasm to call on large companies?

As I was writing this chapter, I found that some principles are more common than others. It would be interesting to survey a larger sample of sales executives and learn which principles are most common to them. I gathered only about ten "win" stories, but even in that small sample I found some principles were common to almost every story. This small sample is diverse and includes different solutions and customer industries. Principles 1, 3, 8, 9, and 10 showed up again and again.

It could be that these principles are common practice, or perhaps they are more essential, or it could be they are the most effective and therefore tied to a win. Principle 1 is so organic to the sale that it must be involved in almost every large account transaction. The only way to win a large account without leveraging Principle 1 would be to somehow have a large opportunity fall in your lap and have the prospect tell you how to complete the sale. Principle 3 was common in my sample, perhaps due to common practice, or it could be that there are benefits in a greater understanding of our prospect's shared interests. I was surprised to see Principle 8 in so many win stories. We knew that more and more people are involved in the buying process, but what we find in these case studies is that the salesperson needs to actively leverage multiple relationships throughout the sale in order to save and grow the sale. I was not surprised to see Principle 9 in every story. Salespeople who do not have some type of consistent prospecting method do not survive or produce. Principle 10 is so important to recognize, especially for salespeople moving from SMB sales into large account sales. It comes up throughout these narratives because success in large accounts comes from using your time wisely.

CONCLUSION

The principles of prospecting to large accounts work like a pyramid, in that you need a foundation to be successful in prospecting and you build upon that foundation to create a pinnacle. Successfully creating quality opportunities is the pinnacle we are after. You greatly increase your chances of reaching this pinnacle when you take steps that get you to the pinnacle.

- *Foundation* – You need a strong foundation in understanding the value and applications of your solution. The greater your mastery, the more you can tailor to each prospect and effectively pivot your approach.

    If you are somewhat new to the solution you are providing, you might invest some time in educating yourself on your solution.

- *Level Two: Choosing Prospects* – Choosing the right prospects can determine your degree of success. If most of the accounts you are calling on are not a great fit for your solution, you will be wasting your invaluable time prospecting to them. If, however, there is a fit, you will know because you'll have more success setting meetings and you will see more interest from your prospects.

- *Level Three: Research* – When you've done a fantastic job with the foundation and level two of our pyramid, you can probably get away with less research. However, investing time learning details about your prospects will help a great deal when it comes time to set meetings. When you know who you're calling on and why you are calling on those contacts,and when you are leading with something relevant to thosecontacts, which you develop as a result of research, you will set more meetings.

- *Pinnacle: Successful Prospecting* – In SMB sales, we are often asked to just make the calls—not even referring to a prospect's website. In large account prospecting, you are not ready to make a call until the foundation of your approach, who you are calling on and why, is established.

In large account prospecting, you need to *have a reason to call* other than you want to sell something. Your reason for calling is based in how you can help your prospect. It takes work in the three levels supporting prospecting to establish that reason for calling.

LANDING NEW ENTERPRISE ACCOUNTS IS HARD, BUT YOU WILL SUCCEED

Establishing a new customer in the enterprise space is hard. It is often a multi-year process. It may take you years of following a company and calling on the right people before you get a real opportunity with them. You may go a couple of weeks of heavy prospecting without finding new opportunities. You could work on an opportunity for many months, or even years, just to lose it in the end.

Yet, success in large account prospecting happens every day and you can experience that success. Bringing in just one large account can turbocharge your career. Your next call could be the one that creates the big opportunity. It is often during dry spells, when you are making contacts, disqualifying prospects, and learning about prospects and your industry, that you are making the progress which pays off down the road.

Prospecting to large accounts will lead to success. You will get a return call that leads to a huge commission. You will follow up with that contact that had zero interest in displacing the incumbent, and they will be happy you called and ready to talk because things changed. Your biggest prospect will have a personnel change, and that new contact will like your approach and want to talk with you. Your next call could change your career.

You will be successful calling on large accounts. Through your understanding and application of your solution, identification of appropriate prospects, research of those prospects and effective, professional prospecting, you will win large accounts. Someone must win them. Why not you?

ENDNOTES

1   Jeff Thull, *Mastering the Complex Sale: How to Compete and Win When the Stakes Are High!*, 2nd ed. (Hoboken, NJ: John WIley & Sons, 2010), 98.

2   Nicholas A.C. Read, *Target Opportunity Selling: Top Sales Performers Reveal What Really Works* (New York, NY: McGraw-Hill Education, 2014), 41.

3   "Customer Buying Behavior," The Challenger, February 21, 2020, https://www.challengerinc.com/customer-buying-behavior/.

4   Nicholas A.C. Read, Target Opportunity Selling: Top Sales Performers Reveal What Really Works (New York, NY: McGraw-Hill Education, 2014), 23-24.

5   Mike Weinberg, *New Sales. Simplified: the Essential Handbook for Prospecting and New Business Development* (American Management Association, 2013), 182.

6   Alexandra Samuel, "I've Worked From Home for 22 Years. Here's What I've Learned," The Wall Street Journal (Dow Jones & Company, March 30, 2020), https://www.wsj.com/articles/ive-worked-from-home-for-22-years-heres-what-ive-learned-11585354640.

7   Neil Rackham and Richard Ruff, *Managing Major Sales: Practical Strategies for Improving Sales Effectiveness* (New York, NY: HarperBusiness, 1991), 30.

8   Rackham and Ruff, 31

9   Jill Konrath, *Selling to Big Companies* (Chicago, IL: Kaplan Publishing, 2016), 41.

10 Ibid.

11 "Outliers (Book)," Wikipedia (Wikimedia Foundation, October 8, 2012), https://en.wikipedia.org/wiki/Outliers.

12 Zig Ziglar and Tom Ziglar, *Born to Win: Find Your Success Code* (Issaquah, WA: Made For Success Publishing, 2017), 103.

13   Brian Williams, "21 Mind-Blowing Sales Stats," Smarter Sales Enablement Blog (The Brevet Group), accessed March 13, 2021, https://blog.thebrevetgroup.com/21-mind-blowing-sales-stats.

14   Marketo.com, "What Is Lead Nurturing?," Marketo.com (Marketo, An Adobe Company, September 16, 2019), https://www.marketo.com/lead-nurturing/.

15   Cass R. Sunstein and Richard H. Thaler, *Nudge: Improving Decisions About Health, Wealth and Happiness* (London, UK: Penguin, 2009), 19.

16   Marc Benioff, *Trailblazer: the Power of Business as the Greatest Platform for Change* (New York, NY: Simon & Schuster, 2020), 37–43.

17   Daniel Pink, *To Sell Is Human: The Surprising Truth About Moving Others* (New York, NY: Riverhead Books, 2013), 122.

18   Pink, 125

19   Matthew Dixon and Brent Adamson, *The Challenger Sale: Taking Control of the Customer Conversation* (New York, NY: Portfolio/Penguin, 2011).

20   Dixon, Adamson, 18

21   Dixon, Adamson, 3

22   Weinberg, 78–79

23   John Medina, "Brain Rule Rundown: Rule #4: We Don't Pay Attention to Boring Things," Brain Rules (John Medina), accessed March 13, 2021, http://www.brain-rules.net/attention.

24   Perry Marshall, *80/20 Sales and Marketing: The Definitive Guide to Working Less and Making More* (New York, NY: Entrepeneur Press, 2013), 29.

25   Marshall, 23–30

26   Ago Cluytens, "3 Proven Ways To Get In Front Of Decision Makers," LinkedIn, January 12, 2017, https://www.linkedin.com/pulse/3-proven-ways-get-front-decision-makers-ago-cluytens.

27   Jeb Blount, *Fanatical Prospecting: The Ultimate Guide for Starting Sales Conversations and Filling the Pipeline by Leveraging Social Selling, Telephone, E-Mail, and Cold Calling* (Hoboken, NJ: Wiley, 2015), 14.

28   Konrath, 139

29   Read, Bistritz, 100

30   Konrath, 139

31   Read, Bistritz, 100

32   Blount, 237–244

33   Paul Petrone, "9 Stats That Will Help You Write Better LinkedIn InMails," LinkedIn, December 22, 2015, https://business.linkedin.com/talent-solutions/blog/linkedin-best-practices/2015/9-stats-that-will-help-you-write-better-linkedin-inmails.

34 Konrath, 139

35 Read, Bistritz, 100

36 Ibid.

37 Weinberg, 61

ACKNOWLEDGMENTS

Writing a book is laborious and could have overwhelmed me if not for the education I received in the English and Philosophy departments at Colorado State University. I had some great years there and grew immensely under the tutelage of many people. William Marvin demanded excellence in writing and reading, and helped me build foundations in those disciplines. Paul Trembath inspired me by introducing me to new ways of looking at the world.

I may never have written this book without encouragement from Coach Grant Melbye. Grant helped me develop and rationalize the concept of this book. Without those initial steps, this book may have stayed but an idea.

Miles Herman and Crit DeMent gave me the guidance and support I needed to grow in large account sales. Their patience, kindness, and direction have made a huge impact on my career. I am honored to have worked with them.

The period of my life when I wrote this book was challenged with health problems and nobody helped me through that more than my wife, Lauren Hemphill. She put my needs before her own and developed a patience with me and kindness toward me for which I will be eternally grateful. Thank you, LoLo, for helping me get through this crazy life.

APPENDIX

The following are bulleted lists from the text, which I thought youmay find useful to refer to as snapshot points of reference. Here are also tables for lead intel and in-person prospecting

Organize Your Prospect Data. Fields You Might Include Are:

- Personal, professional, and transactional history
- Products
- Why they are a top prospect
- Geography
- Size indicators
- Win strategy
- Key people
- Events
- Incumbents
- New products, services, and solution changes
- Company culture
- Goals
- Media
- Notes

Organize Your Research On Contacts.
Fields You Might Include Are:

- Time in current role
- Time at company
- Work history
- Alignment with professional organizations historically and today
- Shared contacts with you and members of your team
- Education background and geographical history
- Hobbies and other personal interests

Why Prospect?

- Opportunities that yield wins
- Opportunities that yield leverage
- A bigger network
- Control over your career
- Control over your income

Other Positive Outcomes From Prospecting Into Select Accounts:

- Gain knowledge
- Meet someone at the prospect company and build rapport
- Disqualify a prospect
- Disqualify a contact
- Find the best decision maker
- Find the incumbent(s)
- Get practice
- Develop your messaging
- Plant seeds

Consultative Reasons To Call A Prospect:

- A different way of thinking about your solution
- Reconfigure or use your solution in a different way
- Fill a need that is new to the world or industry
- Reduce spend
- Increase revenue
- Reduce the amount of time it takes to review data
- Increase available capital
- Increase workflow efficiency
- Reduce the spend of a given solution

Opportunities From Prospecting At Trade Shows:

- Meet people who can introduce you to your ultimate sponsor
- Big value by attending and not exhibiting
- Everyone in one place
- Gain industry knowledge
- Gain prospect knowledge
- Gain advantage over competition
- Pre-show information

Other Platforms At Which To Prospect:

- Company events
- Speaker events
- Charity events
- Industry socials
- Drop offs

Prospect Data Table

Company	Solution	Geography	Employee Count	People	Incumbents	Events	Notes
ABC, Inc.	Accounting Firm	CA	688	Our controller used to work there	Competitor 1 handles is their BI software	Sponsoring Accounting Summit in March	See if our controller can make an introduction. May make sense to attend accounting summit.

Trade Show Prospect Data Table

Exhibitor	Solution	Booth #	Employee Count	Priority	Goals	Notes	Show Notes
ABC, Inc.	Accounting Firm	W1608	688	Y	Meet new decision makers	Incumbent is ABC firm, per VP of Ops in 2017	VP of sales says they still use ABC firm but the sales org hates it. He wants a demo!

ABOUT THE AUTHOR

S am is a Sales and Business Development leader in the technology and finance industries. He has been selling to and developing partnerships with large enterprises since 2011. Before starting his professional career, Sam graduated with honors and was the student commencement speaker of his College of Liberal Arts at Colorado State University.

Printed in Great Britain
by Amazon

39719579R00076